PUBLICATION NUMBER 5

Duke University Commonwealth-Studies Center

The Higher Public Service of the Commonwealth of Australia

The Higher Public Service
of the
Commonwealth of Australia

Howard A. Scarrow

PUBLISHED FOR THE

Duke University Commonwealth-Studies Center

DUKE UNIVERSITY PRESS, DURHAM, N. C.

©1957, Duke University Press

Library of Congress Catalogue Card number 57-13024

Second Printing, 1968

Printed in the United States of America

FOREWORD

ONE OF THE KEY groups in the study of the power structure of any political system is the bureaucracy. Stripped of the insidious connotations sometimes associated with the term, the bureaucracy possibly represents for comparative purposes the most distinctive, indentifiable, and significant group meriting attention by the political scientist. Nevertheless, aside from studies which have been made of the bureaucracies of the United States and of the states of Western Europe, relatively little attention has been given to this "core group" in other countries. It is for this reason that the study of "The Higher Public Service of the Commonwealth of Australia" by Dr. Howard A. Scarrow is to be welcomed. It adds both to the scanty literature on the Australian civil service and provides a case study on bureaucracy in a modern democratic state on which to base comparisons of political systems in the future.

As Dr. Scarrow indicates, the Australian civil service, though influenced by the British example, has acquired distinctive features of its own. He traces the growth of the "Commonwealth Public

Service" in the light of the expanded role of government in Australia and examines the evolution of the machinery of personnel administration. The development, composition, and growth of the higher public service is the center on which his research work has been focused. From this study some picture of the role of the bureaucracy in policy planning and formulation, pressures exerted by certain groups at the national level on it, and the competing loyalties and ultimate responsibility of the bureaucrat emerges.

Dr. Scarrow, now Assistant Professor of Political Science at Michigan State University, spent some eighteen months in Australia collecting the data for this volume. His published research on certain aspects of both Australian and Canadian bureaucracy has appeared in several professional journals in Australia, the United Kingdom, and the United States. During the years 1955-1957 he served as Executive Secretary of the Duke University Commonwealth-Studies Center.

The Commonwealth-Studies Center was created in 1955 through the generous financial support of the Carnegie Corporation. Since the Center is concerned exclusively with the encouragement of research, any interpretations of Commonwealth developments appearing in its publications do not represent expressions of the views of the Carnegie Corporation or of the Center; the authors of the several publications are responsible for the conclusions expressed in them.

R. TAYLOR COLE

PREFACE

THE IMPORTANCE of the bureaucracy in the modern state offers clear justification for its close examination. In Australia, as a nation in which approximately one out of every five of the working population is employed by a public authority, government employees perform a role which is especially significant. The purpose of the following study is to examine one segment of the Australian bureaucracy, the higher ranks of the federal or Commonwealth Public Service.[1] Attention will be centered upon its development, composition, and role, and upon the machinery of personnel administration from which it has evolved. The study is primarily an analysis of major developments and trends; and while numerous prob-

---

[1] In Australia the term "Commonwealth" is used in three separate contexts. Usually it is used as a synonym for "federal," e.g., the Commonwealth government. It may also refer to the whole of Australia. Finally it may be used in reference to the British Commonwealth of Nations. In this study the term is used almost exclusively to refer to the federal or central government.

lems which confront the Service are discussed, no attempt has been made to suggest possible solutions.

Some of the material, particularly in the introductory chapter, has been included in order to acquaint the American reader with major background considerations. It is hoped that the volumes which are cited in the footnotes may serve to suggest sources of more complete information and discussion.

In accordance with Australian usage, the term "public service" has been used in preference to "civil service." Reference to the Commonwealth Public Service includes all personnel employed under the terms of the Public Service Acts of 1902 and 1922. It is not intended to cover Commonwealth employees hired under other legislation.

The comprehensive study by Robert S. Parker, *Public Service Recruitment in Australia,*[2] which discusses the public services of the six Australian states and the Commonwealth, has influenced the selection of the background material included in Chapter 2. Major stress has been accorded to developments not covered in that volume, especially since 1945. Events during the period of World War II have been touched upon only as they may relate to later developments. Most of the material has been amended to include the period through 1955, although certain data in Chapter 4 is as of an earlier date, as indicated.

I am pleased to record my indebtedness to the United States Educational Foundation, Canberra, for the Fulbright grant awarded in March, 1952, and

[2] Melbourne, 1942.

subsequently extended, which made possible the field research on which this study is based. To its Executive Officer, Mr. Geoffrey Rossiter, who cordially assisted me in numerous ways, I owe special thanks. I also wish to acknowledge a deep sense of appreciation for the courteous assistance of many Australians in the preparation of this study. I am very much indebted to Mr. W. E. Dunk, Chairman of the Commonwealth Public Service Board, for his generous co-operation in making available relevant files and materials and in allowing me to pursue my investigations within the Board's office; and to many of his able staff whose cordiality and helpfulness made possible a knowledge of the Service which otherwise would have been denied. Professor L. C. Webb of the Australian National University not only minimized the initial difficulties which confront the overseas visitor, but also continually shared with me his special knowledge of administrative problems. For this I am deeply grateful. I am obliged to L. F. Crisp, Professor of Political Science at Canberra University College, and Gordon Greenwood, Professor of History and Political Science at the University of Queensland, who offered numerous suggestions during the early draft of the manuscript. To Robert S. Parker, Reader in Public Administration at the Australian National University, T. H. Kewley, Senior Lecturer in Government and Public Administration at the University of Sydney, and a senior official (who shall not be named here) of the

Commonwealth Public Service Board, I owe a great debt of gratitude. In reading the manuscript in part or in its entirety, they have saved me from numerous errors of fact and judgment. For all deficiencies which remain I am, of course, solely responsible.

I wish to thank Professor Richard Leach of Duke University and Professor Glendon Schubert of Michigan State University for their many helpful suggestions in improving the style and clarity of presentation. And to Professor R. Taylor Cole of Duke University the debts accrued are many. His stimulating interest in bureaucracy has served as a continuous challenge, and as a result of his encouragement this study was undertaken. Finally, I wish to acknowledge the opportunity of completing the study which has been afforded by my position of Executive Secretary of the Duke University Commonwealth-Studies Center.

HOWARD A. SCARROW

Duke University
April, 1957

CONTENTS

The Higher Public Service of
the Commonwealth of Australia

Introduction

POLITICAL FRAMEWORK

APPROXIMATELY two hundred miles south of Sydney in a broad, natural basin lies the federal capital of Australia. Modeled upon the circular designs of a Chicago landscape architect and populated largely by public servants, Canberra has been described as "six suburbs in search of a city," or, by its more severe critics, as a wholly artificial community in which a restless and isolated bureaucracy runs rampant. Upon his arrival in Canberra the overseas visitor is earnestly cautioned that the capital is in no way representative of the states or the people which voted its creation, and that he must look elsewhere for the real Australia. He may be counseled to visit the state capitals, which together contain over 50 per cent of the total population. Or he may be told that the real Australia is to be found in the outback, in the bush, from whence springs the tradition of "mateship,"[1] regarded by some as the prevailing social

[1]Professor Overacker has equated "mateship" with "respect for the ideas and personality of others, fortitude, genuineness,

ethos underlying Australian democracy. There will be firm agreement, in any event, that the federal capital is not typical of Australia.

Federalism. In spite of these denials and apologies on the part of Australians themselves, Canberra has in fact come to symbolize, both internationally and domestically, the summit of government authority in this South Pacific outpost of the British Commonwealth; and within its boundaries the visitor can see clearly reflected the principal features of the Australian political framework. The very existence of Canberra, which was founded upon interstate jealousies, serves as a constant reminder of what is without doubt the most pervasive political problem besetting Australians, viz., the operation of the federal union.[2] Modeled to a large extent upon the United States Constitution, the Australian Constitution Act of 1900 spelled out in Article 51 the specific powers which were to be the province of the federal government. The states were left with all residual legislative powers. Unlike American practice, however, judicial interpretation by the High

---

and a politeness which springs from the heart rather than the pages of Emily Post." Louise Overacker, *The Australian Party System* (New Haven, 1952), p. 11.

[2] The study of Australian federalism has attracted widespread interest among Australian and overseas scholars. Among the better studies the following may be mentioned: Gordon Greenwood, *The Future of Australian Federalism: A Commentary on the Working of the Constitution* (Melbourne, 1946); Geoffrey Sawer, ed., *Federalism in Australia* (Melbourne, 1949), and *Federalism: An Australian Jubilee Study* (Melbourne, 1952); and Kenneth C. Wheare, *Federal Government* (3rd ed., London, 1953).

Court of Australia has failed to minimize the effects of the legal restrictions imposed upon the central parliament. To be sure, the doctrines of "implied limitations" and "implied prohibitions," earnestly propounded by the three original members of the court, were buried by judicial decision in 1920;[3] and subsequent decisions have tended to strengthen the position of the Commonwealth. Nevertheless, by virtue of certain judicial doctrines, in particular the limitation placed upon federal action in the field of interstate commerce, Australian constitutional development has not been easily reconciled with the requirements of an advanced industrial democracy. Nor has the formal amending process been effectively utilized in adjusting the division of powers to present needs. As a result of a complex amending process (similar to the Swiss), only four amendments to the Constitution have been approved by the electorate, and of these only one added to the enumerated powers granted to the Commonwealth.

Largely because of this rigid legal structure, the question of striking a satisfactory balance between the Commonwealth and the states has remained the subject of lively debate, and the problems raised by the federal system constantly obtrude themselves into the political arena. As late as 1934 secession was a prominent issue in Western Australia, and the "new states movement" still claims scattered support. The machinery of federal-state co-operation has become a conspicuous part of the established political in-

[3] *Engineer's Case* (1920), 28 C.L.R. 129.

stitutions, and meetings of the Premiers' Conference and other joint consultative councils nearly always command headlines in the nation's press. Although through these co-operative arrangements significant progress has been made, delays, uncertainties, and outright disagreements have retarded their usefulness. In the field of marketing, for example, the need for complete federal control is especially apparent, and in 1946 even such a seemingly innocuous project as standardizing railway gauges was rejected by two states.

However, the decisive round in the constitutional struggle has possibly been won by the Commonwealth, for in 1942 the High Court approved a uniform taxation scheme whereby the Commonwealth collects all income taxes. The court not only held that the legislation was constitutional, but also held that its legality was not dependent upon the wartime emergency and that the Commonwealth could make its reimbursement grants to the states contingent upon any conditions which it cared to stipulate.[4] Thus, legally at least, the Commonwealth is now in a position to upset the federal structure. The states, in contrast, although relieved of the politically unpopular task of imposing heavy taxes, are forced to draw up their budgets according to the size of the grant they hope to receive from Canberra.[5]

[4] *Uniform Tax Case* (1942), 65 C.L.R. 373.
[5] "The Prime Minister expressed the relative financial position of the federation and the states at the Premiers' Conference of January 1946, when he brusquely informed the state Premiers that the single Commonwealth income tax would be continued

Parliamentary Institutions. For several months out of the year political attention in Canberra is focused upon Parliament House. Here is a bicameral legislature perpetuates the tradition of parliamentary self-government and cabinet responsibility inherited from the United Kingdom.[6] Distinguished from the British Parliament in that its authority is limited by the specific terms of a federal constitution, the Commonwealth Parliament is composed of a House of Representatives and a Senate. Members of the House serve for three years, while the term of a senator is six years. Half of the senators from each state retire every three years. The Constitution provides that the size of the House must be "as nearly as practicable" twice the size of the Senate, and until 1948 this relation was maintained in the ratio of 75 to 36 (six senators from each state). Legislation introduced in 1948 greatly increased these figures, so that by 1955 they stood at 124 and 60, respectively.

Both houses are chosen by direct popular election.

---

indefinitely, and described their unanimous objections as 'all ————nonsense.' " Geoffrey Sawer, *Australian Government Today* (4th ed., Melbourne, 1954), p. 8.

[6] Comparatively little has been written on the political institutions of the Commonwealth. The most extensive treatments are to be found in L. F. Crisp, *The Parliamentary Government of the Commonwealth of Australia* (New Haven, 1949), and J. B. D. Miller, *Australian Government and Politics: An Introductory Survey* (London, 1954). Briefer descriptions are contained in Geoffrey Sawer, *Australian Government Today* (4th ed., Melbourne, 1954), and Alexander Brady, *Democracy in the Dominions: A Comparative Study of Institutions* (2nd ed., Toronto, 1952), chap. viii.

Registration and voting are compulsory, and penalties are effectively enforced. The voting system used for the House of Representatives is the simple preferential vote, but since 1948 the Senate has been elected by a method of proportional representation.

The Senate, planned after the American upper chamber, was intended by the founding fathers to embody the federal principle of state representation. Rigid party discipline, however, has worked largely to frustrate this objective, and state interests are no more adequately represented in the Senate than in the lower house. What makes the Senate more than a mere reviewing body, however, is the possibility that it may contain a majority hostile to the Government in power. Although the Cabinet is responsible only to the House of Representatives, the Senate, as a fully co-ordinate branch of Parliament (except in the passage of money bills) is always in a position to block Government measures; and because only half of the senators retire every three years deadlocks are easily possible. Nevertheless, on only two occasions has the double dissolution machinery been employed to resolve these conflicts.[7]

Nowhere in the Constitution is explicit mention made of the Cabinet, the Prime Minister, or the presuppositions underlying responsible cabinet government. Instead the usual conventions of parliamentary democracy are relied upon much as in Westminster.

[7] The first was in 1914 and resulted in the defeat of the Government. The second, in 1951, ended in another victory for the Liberal-Country Coalition Government.

The executive government as sketched in the Constitution is composed of the Queen's representative—the Governor-General—and the Federal Executive Council. The latter, which advises the Governor-General "in the government of the Commonwealth," is composed of the officers appointed by the Governor-General to administer the various departments and are "the Queen's Ministers of State." Although it is as members of the Executive Council that cabinet ministers take their oath of office, the Executive Council is in fact a purely formal body which satisfies certain legal requirements. In recent years "there have rarely been more than the necessary two or three Commonwealth ministers present at a Commonwealth Executive Council meeting."[8] All ministers must be members of Parliament, and until 1956 there were no ministers outside the Cabinet. Following his Government's last victory at the polls in 1955, Prime Minister Menzies introduced a ministry modeled after British practice. It is composed of twelve cabinet ministers and nine junior ministers outside the Cabinet.

The Governor-General is appointed by the Queen upon the recommendation of the Prime Minister and holds office for a limited period (usually about five years). In keeping with the Imperial Conference Report of 1926, his relation to the Commonwealth Parliament is generally identical with that of the Queen to the Parliament at Westminster, and his

[8] Crisp, p. 194.

powers are defined by the same conventions. With
two exceptions (in 1931 and 1946) the Governor-
General has been a titled Englishman. Both of
these exceptional appointments were recommended
by Labour Governments, and each aroused widespread criticism. The appointment of Mr. William
J. McKell as Governor-General by the Chifley
Labor Government in 1946 is reported to have
"rocked the Commonwealth to its foundations. . . .
His appointment was challenged on the ground that
he was an active Labor partisan at the time of his
appointment. It was clear, also, that his humble
social origins shocked many, and in the battle of
words over his appointment 'no stone was left un-
thrown.' "[9]

Political Parties. The members who converge
upon Canberra when Parliament is in session are
representatives of three political parties: the Australian Labour party (ALP), the Liberal party, and
the Country party.[10] Professor Louise Overacker
has described these parties, in contrast with those
of the United States, as having developed "shells
as hard as any mollusks in the political zoo."[11] Discipline is tight, members are expected to pay dues and
attend meetings, "and candidates, elected representatives, and even the rank-and-file membership are

[9] Overacker, p. 22 n. 46.
[10] The only complete treatment of Australian political parties
is Louise Overacker, *The Australian Party System* (New Haven,
1952). Another recent and valuable analysis is S. R. Davis *et
al., The Australian Political Party System* (Sydney, 1954).
[11] Overacker, p. 1.

part of a unified organization with an avowed national program and a recognized leadership."[12] The nonconformist, within Parliament and without, runs the risk of expulsion. Australian parties are private associations, recognized neither in the Constitution nor in statute law, and selection of candidates is strictly the concern of the party.

Broadly speaking, the major parties represent three distinct economic groupings. The strength of the ALP is founded largely on the trade-union movement, although organized labor and the Labour party are by no means synonymous. The party's roots date back to 1891, and while doctrinal unity has never been achieved, the ALP has continuously stood to the left of the other major parties. The Liberal party, formed in 1944, has harnessed the support of the manufacturing, banking, and merchant interests previously identified first with the Nationalist party, and later with the United Australia party. Since its creation, however, the new Liberal party has sought to propagate a doctrine of constructive "liberalism," and the "old negativism and defeatism have given away to what may develop into a middle-class dynamic."[13] The Country party gains its support primarily from farmers and graziers, although its leaders have been representative of other conservative interests. The party plays an important part in national politics, not because of its size, but rather as

[12] *Ibid.*, p. 2. These generalizations apply in particular to the ALP.
[13] *Ibid.*, p. 326.

a result of its strategic position. Without its support the Liberal party would be unable to secure the necessary majority to form a government.

Political historians normally refer to the political struggle in Australia in terms of Labour versus anti-Labour. It is generally agreed that both in organization and in program the ALP has wielded a determining influence upon the complexion of Australian political life. But for success at the national level, the ALP has found it difficult to combat the alliance of the two conservative parties, and as of August, 1941, Labour had held office for only seven years and two months during the forty-year span of Commonwealth history.[14]   From August, 1941, until the general election of 1949, Labour, under the leadership of John Curtin (1941-45) and J. B. Chifley (1945-49), successfully guided the country through one of the most challenging periods of its history, only to be swept from office in April, 1949, by the Menzies-Fadden, Liberal-Country Coalition. Similar defeats were inflicted upon Labour in 1951, following the double dissolution of Parliament, again in 1954, and again in December, 1955. A bad split in the Labour party, now led by Dr. H. V. Evatt, is as least partially responsible for its most recent reverses.

Administrative Background

Like the other government institutions already described, the Commonwealth administrative struc-

[14] C. Hartley Grattan, *Introducing Australia* (New York, 1942), p. 154.

ture was formally created on January 1, 1901. Its importance had been underscored by the deliberate decision of the founders of the federation that the central government would operate directly on the people, rather than through the states.

Among the important enactments of the first Parliament was the Public Service Act of 1902.[15] By the turn of the century the antipatronage principles underlying the Northcote-Trevelyan Report had become generally accepted by the Australian Colonies. Open and competitive examinations conducted by independent authorities and the idea of a career service free from political influences were established traditions. The framers of the first public service legislation, therefore, were able to construct a system which was creative, rather than reformative, and also were in the favorable position of being able to take advantage of colonial experience. They borrowed heavily from the public service legislation which had been enacted in the colonies, especially the larger ones of Victoria and New South Wales. Complete control over both staffing and departmental establishment was vested in a single Commissioner, appointed by the Governor-General and holding office for seven years. It has been observed that the 1902 Act constituted the most advanced

[15] Act No. 5, 1902. From Jan. 1, 1901, until the Public Service Act came into force in 1903 all appointments to the Public Service were made by the Governor-General in Council under the terms of Section 67 of the Constitution.

legislation of its kind in Australia[16] and, it could be added, in its coverage was far ahead of civil service enactments in other democracies, such as Canada or the United States.

For nearly twenty years the 1902 legislation served as the basis of public service administration. In 1918 the then retired first Commissioner, Mr. D. C. McLachlan, was appointed to inquire into the administration of the Public Service[17] and partly as a result of his findings—but by no means wholly reflecting them—completely new public service legislation was enacted in 1922.[18] The McLachlan Royal Commission and the resulting Public Service Act of 1922 mark the last major attempt to investigate and strengthen the Commonwealth Public Service. Since that date any form of parliamentary inquiry, except for limited investigations by the Public Accounts Committee, seems to have been scrupulously avoided and, in consequence, the content of public service legislation has remained, with a few important exceptions, essentially unaltered.

Public Service Board. One of the significant changes introduced by the 1922 Act was the creation of a three-member Board of Commissioners, headed by a chairman, in which were vested powers similar to those formerly exercised by the Commissioner. The departure from single commissioner control had

---

[16] Robert S. Parker, *Public Service Recruitment in Australia* (Melbourne, 1942), p. 31.

[17] *Report of Royal Commission on Public Service Administration* (1920). Hereinafter cited as *Royal Commission Report.*

[18] Act No. 21, 1922.

been opposed by McLachlan, and reflected instead the influence of the Royal Commission on Economies, a body constituted at the end of World War I to investigate public expenditures. Beginning in 1930, however, the Government failed to appoint new Commissioners as vacancies occurred, with the results that from 1931 to 1945 the Service reverted to control by a single Commissioner. The Board, which since 1947 has operated at full strength, is presently composed of two former permanent heads, both of whom have spent their careers in the Commonwealth Service, and a former New South Wales official recruited to the Commonwealth Service in 1948.

The Public Service Board has been entrusted with wide powers and responsibilities. These not only cover matters relating directly to personnel, but also extend to broader matters of administration. Any increase in departmental establishment, raise in classification, or change in organization must first be investigated and approved by the Board.[19] Investigations are also conducted to improve departmental efficiency, a function familiarly titled "O and M," although statutory authority to enforce the resulting recommendations is lacking.[20] In brief, the Board

[19] The Parliamentary Joint Committee of Public Accounts has questioned the effectiveness of the Board's control over establishment, since the authorized number of positions is often substantially in excess of the actual staff employed. See its *Fifteenth Report* (1954), p. 43.

[20] See Public Service Act (1922), Sec. 17. As a result of this limitation responsibility for departmental efficiency is actually divided between the Board and the departments.

is much more than a central personnel agency; it is a major authority controlling administration. During the operation of the 1902 Public Service Act the extensive powers given to the Commissioner were never fully utilized, and he and his limited staff devoted their major attention to the detailed problems of personnel control, many of which had resulted from the amalgamation of sections of the state services. It was this failure to exercise broader control which prompted the Royal Commission on Economies to recommend the creation of a Board of Commissioners whose major interest was to be "business management." Effective control over organization and methods has, however, been in evidence only since the Board reached full strength in 1947. The Board now employs over 300 officers (three times the number in 1946), who are stationed in Canberra and the six capital cities.

By means of the usual safeguards of definite tenure and protected salary, the Board occupies a status independent of political control; and on occasion it has used its freedom to call attention to irregularities or to certain administrative policies of the Government with which it is in disagreement (e.g., absolute preference for veterans). On the whole, however, the Board is an integral part of the administrative machinery whose effectiveness is dependent in large measure upon relationships established with the departments and the Government. Not surprisingly, moreover, the Board shares certain authority with other agencies. In scrutinizing the annual draft estimates the Treasury can question proposed departmental expenditure and the size of establishments.[21] The Treasury must also agree that funds are available for new positions authorized by the Board; and while this approval is usually forthcoming, the Treasury is able to examine the proposals and to question them.

It is the Cabinet or Prime Minister, moreover, which distributes the administrative functions among the various departments and ultimately determines the nature and limits of departmental activity. One result of political control over departmental jurisdiction has been frequent changes in the administrative arrangements, fluctuations in the number and titles of departments, and sometimes an anomalous division of functions. An official war historian recalls that the creation of the Department of Civil Aviation in 1938, in lieu of a general Department of Transport as recommended by defense advisers, was rationalized by "reasons related to the comfort of the Cabinet

[21] It is a "standing rule of the Treasury" that provision for new staff is deleted from the draft estimates "unless there are urgent reasons to the contrary." See Joint Committee of Public Accounts, *Eighteenth Report* (1954), p. 20. The role of the Treasury appears to have increased considerably in recent years. One permanent secretary speaks of "the joyous struggles of a Permanent Head in organisation, management and staffing matters which nowadays seem to involve him with the Treasury hardly less than with the Public Service Board." See J. G. Crawford, "The Role of the Permanent Head," *Public Administration*, journal of the Australian Regional Groups of the Royal Institute of Public Administration, Sept., 1954, p. 153.

Hereinafter, unless otherwise noted, reference to *Public Administration* denotes the journal of the Australian Regional Groups.

rather than the needs of administration."[22]   The
Public Service Board pointed to perhaps a more
serious anomaly when it suggested in its 1951 report
that the health benefit scheme could be more economically administered by the Department of Social Services than by the Health Department.[23]

The other important limitation of the Board's
jurisdiction is the Public Service Arbitrator, who
settles disputes and registers agreements between the
numerous staff associations and the Public Service
Board.   It should be emphasized that labor conditions in the entire Australian economy are controlled
by judgments of Commonwealth or state arbitration courts, and that the wage structure is based upon
the court determination of the amount of the "basic
wage" and of "margins" awarded for skill.   In
cases brought before him, the Public Service Arbitrator determines the appropriate "margin" for positions

[22] Paul Hasluck, *The Government and the People, 1939-1941*
(Canberra, 1952), p. 467 n. 3.

[23] *Twenty-Seventh Report* (1951), p. 8.   The distribution
of administrative functions is formally enumerated in the Administrative Arrangements Order, a document prepared by the Prime
Minister's Department and issued by the Governor-General.
However, the exact significance and authority of this document
have been questioned.   See Joint Committee of Public Accounts,
Third Report (1953).

In the opinion of one senior public servant neither the Board,
the Treasury, nor the Prime Minister's Department "operates in
such a way as to be regarded as the head of the Public Service.
Right at the top there is a vacuum of responsibility." Looking to
the example of the United Kingdom, he suggests that the Service
"would benefit by having someone who was recognised as its
leader and who would thus fill this vacuum." See B. W. Hartnell, "Power and Responsibility in the Commonwealth Public
Service," *Public Administration*, Sept., 1955, p. 143.

in the Public Service, salary relativities of the different positions, and other conditions of employment. The majority of negotiations between the Board and the staff associations end in agreement, a notable exception being the "margins" dispute of 1955 which was settled only after the Board appealed to the Commonwealth Arbitration Court against a judgment of the Public Service Arbitrator.[24]

In summary, while the wide powers vested in the Public Service Board distinguish Australian from British practice, these powers are limited in several significant ways. Attention will now be focused on the public service machinery administered by the Board, as it has developed through legislation and practice.

[24] The "margins" awarded amounted to about half those initially determined by the Arbitrator, but still added a total of about two million pounds to the government annual wage bill. For a history of public service arbitration procedures see Leo Blair, "Arbitration in the Federal Public Service of Australia," *Public Administration*, journal of the Royal Institute of Public Administration, Spring, 1956, pp. 61-73.

2

The Machinery Governing the Composition of the Higher Public Service

IN THIS CHAPTER certain of the legal provisions and administrative practices which have determined the composition of the higher Public Service will be examined. These will be discussed under the following headings: Classification; Recruitment; Promotion; Post-entry Training; and Salaries.

CLASSIFICATION

Like other Commonwealth countries, e.g., Canada and South Africa, Australia has adopted a classification scheme under which each post is separately graded. Although the phraseology of the Public Service Act is rather ambiguous on this point, in practice it is the position—identified by a detailed statement of duties and an appropriate title—which is the object of classification, rather than the individual officer. The theory of position classification should not conceal the fact that often, particularly at the higher levels, an officer's merit can determine the classification of his position; and in the External

Affairs Department the system actually operates in such a way as to give diplomatic officers a personal rank much the same as in the British or United States Foreign Service. Nevertheless, the entire administration of the Service is premised upon the position as being the basic unit of classification.

Divisional Classification. Each position in the Public Service is classified in two ways, by division and by salary scale. The Public Service Act of 1902 separated the Service into four divisions: Administrative, Professional, Clerical, and General. To be included in the first were all permanent heads and chief officers (the head departmental officers in each state), and also persons recommended by the Commissioner. The Professional Division was to comprise officers whose duties necessitated "some special skill or technical knowledge usually acquired only in some profession or occupation different from the ordinary routine of the Public Service." The composition of the Clerical and General Division was to be left to the discretion of the Commissioner.

The Public Service Act of 1922 introduced two significant changes in the divisional classification. The first was an amalgamation of the Professional and Clerical Divisions. In his *Royal Commission Report,* McLachlan stated that numerous anomalies had resulted from the distinction between "Clerical" and "Professional." Officers were to be found in the Professional Division "whose duties could not even under a most liberal interpretation be considered as professional in character."[1] They had been so classified in order to overcome the examination barrier or age restriction, in order that higher salaries might be paid, or because it was considered "injudicious" to classify them in the Administrative Division. Rather than recommend that the composition of the two divisions be more closely regulated, McLachlan questioned the justification of distinguishing between them. The original purpose of the separation, he reasoned, had been that the conditions of entrance to the two divisions had not been the same. The Act had prescribed separate entrance examinations to the Professional, Clerical, and General Divisions; and appointment without examination, under certain special circumstances, was allowed only to the administrative and professional offices. In the opinion of the former Commissioner, conditions of entrance to both the Professional and Clerical Divisions should be identical, viz., normally by competitive examination; and appointment without examination to positions requiring special skill and training should be allowed to both the professional and the clerical ranks.

The second departure from the original divisional classification scheme introduced by the 1922 legislation was the abandonment of descriptive nomenclature in favor of numerical designation; for McLachlan had argued that the old titles (Administrative, Clerical, Professional, and General) has given rise to "an irritating distinction of 'caste.' "[2]

[1] *Royal Commission Report*, p. 36.
[2] *Ibid.*, p. 37.

In line with his recommendation, therefore, the Public Service Act of 1922 separated the Service into First, Second, Third, and Fourth Divisions. The First Division was to include "all Permanent Heads of Departments and such other officers as the Governor-General determines." The Second Division was to be composed of "officers who, under officers of the First Division, are required to exercise executive or professional functions in the more important offices of the Service." The composition of the Third and Fourth Divisions was to be left to the discretion of the Public Service Board. In practice, however, McLachlan's recommendation that the Third Division represent an amalgamation of most former Clerical and Professional Division officers was adopted; and the Fourth Division continued to cover the manual and manipulative grades (mostly in the Post Office).

Two points may be noted in connection with the altered system of divisional classification. The first is that the First Division is now far more exclusive than the former Administrative Division. Although it is evident from his report, and also from the wording of the Act, that McLachlan had not anticipated this result, the policy of the new Public Service Board was to confine the First Division almost exclusively to heads of departments. Formerly, in addition to permanent heads, the Administrative Division had included the Deputy Postmasters-General and the Collectors of Customs in each state, the Commonwealth Statistician, the Chief Electoral Officer, and certain other senior officials.

Of greater significance is the fact that justification for divisional classification has now largely disappeared. Where formerly the divisions were of use in connection with recruitment methods, the abandonment of Professional and Clerical Divisions in favor of Second and Third Divisions substituted a classification based on the importance of the work for one which had been based on the nature of qualifications required. Thus with the exception of the barrier separating the Third and Fourth Divisions, recruitment methods and divisional classifications are no longer related. Within the range of positions embraced by the First, Second, and Third Divisions—including permanent heads at one end of the scale and base-grade clerks on the other—competitive examinations are conducted solely for entrance to the latter, and nonexamination appointment is allowed to each.

Apart, then, from separating the Fourth Division from the rest of the Service, the present divisional classification serves little practical use. The First Division does little more than reinforce the exclusiveness of officers already singled out by their designation as secretary or permanent head. Second Division status can denote positions ranging from the Deputy Secretary of the Treasury to a Medical Officer in the Health Department, or a relatively junior departmental representative stationed in Hobart; and the salary classifications of officers in the Third Division—even of nonprofessional officers—are sometimes higher than those in the Second Division. Indeed, a single schedule of salary scales applies to both Second and Third Division officers. All that can be said, therefore, is that the First, Second, and Third Divisions provide a convenient designation for officers in rather broad and overlapping salary and occupational groups. And although these divisions are usually said to equate roughly with the British Administrative, Executive, and Clerical Classes, they form a single pyramid, rather than three separate ones. The absence of qualification barriers, combined with the emphasis on filling higher positions by promotion from below, renders them useless as recruitment and promotion aids.

By June, 1955, the permanent officers of the Service were classified as follows:[3]

First Division	29
Second Division	315
Third Division	28,269
Fourth Division	53,717
TOTAL	82,330

Classification within Divisions. Under provisions of the Public Service Act of 1902 classification within divisions was based upon numerical or alphabetical designation. The Clerical Division, for example, was divided into five classes (a "Special" Class was added in 1911), and the schedule of the Act prescribed the minimum and maximum salary as well as the amount of annual increment appropriate to each. It was a

[3] Public Service Board, *Thirty-First Report* (1955), p. 22.

workable arrangement, distinguished by its clarity and simplicity.

As the Service grew larger and more complex, McLachlan became increasingly dissatisfied with this feature of the Public Service Act. The number of classes was insufficient and the salary scales were too rigid. In his *Royal Commission Report*, consequently, the former Commissioner recommended an increase in the number of classes, smaller salary ranges for each, and automatic annual increments—a system intended to reflect more carefully the worth of each position and to relieve the heavy burden on administrative officers in granting discretionary increments.

In general, the new Public Service Board accepted the principle underlying these recommendations, and the new legislation opened the way for a reclassification of the Service. Nevertheless, the Board departed from McLachlan's proposals in one important particular. Rather than adhere to the former system of numerically designated classes, it abandoned class designation completely and simply classified each position by salary scale.[4] Moreover, it was the policy of the Board to draw extremely minute distinctions between the value of positions, to classify each individual position as an independent unit, and to eliminate classes of positions altogether. When it commenced its reclassification of the Service, the Board attempted to extend the principle of minute evaluation to its ultimate limit. Later, however, it modified

[4] Thus the "Fifth Class Clerk" under the 1902 Act became "Clerk £ 90-324."

its policy, and from all the dismembered units of individual classification there emerged a relatively fixed number of standard salary scales, most of them covering a five year span.[5] The determinations by the Public Service Arbitrator appear to have been largely responsible for this retreat, since the original scheme rested on a precarious positional relativity easily upset by a single award.[6]

There remain, however, several disadvantages associated with the present method of classification. The first results from the large number of short and overlapping salary ranges. Because of the limited opportunity offered in a particular position, officers are constantly striving to seek promotion to a new position classified with a higher—although sometimes almost insignificantly higher—maximum salary. The weekly Commonwealth *Gazette*, which contains notifications of vacancies, is zealously scanned by officers searching for promotion opportunities. The consequent time consumed in applying and, if unsuccessful, in appealing, results in frequent disruption

[5] The number of salary scales has recently totaled about thirty for the Second and Third Divisions. This number is not exhaustive, for certain positions are classified at salary ranges not represented in the standard list.

[6] In its 1928 report (p. 5) the Board complained: "Unfortunately much of the work performed in the classification has been rendered nugatory by determinations made during the past year under the Arbitration (Public Service) Act. . . . The scheme of classification, laboriously brought to completion by the Board after some years of patient research and inquiry has been varied by the Court in important details with further increased cost to the Commonwealth and with a disturbance of previous relativity of officers which must affect the stability and contentment of the Service."

of work. The successful applicant, moreover, sometimes spends but a few months in the new position
before being promoted to yet another. Thus the
rate of turnover assumes significant proportions, and
what little experience the officer can gain in a particular line of work is soon lost. The system also results
in situations in which a valuable officer can virtually
blackmail the head of his department into recommending reclassification of his position in order to
prevent his seeking promotion in another section
of the Service. Finally, from the administrative
side, the work and expense involved in the constant
movement of staff results in overburdening the Board
and departmental administrative officers with a maze
of detailed tasks. Most of these objections were
admitted by the Board in its 1947 report. In reply,
however, the Board stressed that "stagnation" must
be avoided and that capable officers should quickly be
able to adapt themselves to various types of positions.[7]

A second difficulty resulting from classification
by salary scale is also apparent. Originally it was
intended that the worth of each position was to be
expressed in meaningful terms of monetary units.
In periods of currency instability, however, it becomes
impossible to maintain the correlation. During the
depression of the thirties, when all Public Service
salaries were reduced under the terms of the Financial
Emergency Act, the prescribed salary scales lost
their significance and became mere descriptive desig-

[7] Public Service Board, *Twenty-Third Report* (1947), p. 10.

nations. More recently, as Australia has experienced a violent inflationary spiral and as all salaries have been increased with each rise in the basic wage, the amount of actual salary paid to an officer has become considerably more than that indicated by the salary range attached to his position. Margins awarded by the Public Service Arbitrator have further increased the discrepancy. By 1951 the relationship had become so completely distorted that special legislation was enacted which attempted to bring the "standard" into line with the "actual." The major purpose was to present the Public Service to potential recruits in more favorable terms. Yet even after 1951 there were significant rises in actual salaries, so that by 1955 another salaries adjustment act was necessary to raise again the standard salary labels.

The third disadvantage associated with the present classification scheme is that the system, as it has evolved, necessitates continuous review by the Public Service Board so that proper and consistent relationships between positions may be maintained. Since 1945 a portion of this task has been assumed by classification committees constituted under legislation enacted in that year. Established at the request of the Public Service associations, these committees are composed of one representative of the Public Service Board (who acts as chairman), one from the department concerned, and one from the appropriate Service association. They conduct sectional classification reviews as conditions warrant.[8] The Board has not

[8] These committees made their contribution during the period

been relieved of its primary responsibility for classification, however, and it is continually being solicited
by departments to grant higher classifications to
positions in their establishments. Just as individual
officers scan the *Gazette* for possible promotion
opportunities, so the permanent heads or administrative officers watch for reclassifications, which are
announced in the same publication. Any alleged
discrimination against their department is usually
met by appeals to the Board. A flow of correspondence or series of discussions with the Public Service
Inspector then ensues, all with the object of determining which position or which type of position is of
greater value. The weakness of the system is most
sharply revealed when departments request reclassification of positions for the sole, yet very legitimate, reason that the occupant has proved himself
to be of greater worth than is allowed by his salary
classification. Usually the request is couched in terms
of increased responsibility which has accrued to the
position, but the real reason is often that the one
occupant imparts to the position an importance which
it would not possess when filled by another officer.
The system allows of no redress short of a complete
position reclassification with all the consequent administrative work involved. Finally, it has been observed
that at the higher levels the differentiated salary

1945-1950 when practically every department underwent a complete reclassification. Their use is now more limited. In effect,
the committees take the arbitration process one step backward by
getting the employee associations to approve classifications before
they are formally registered.

ranges foster "an unnecessarily and dangerously competitive element in some officers' approach to policy
problems."[9]

McLachlan had forseen some of these difficulties
and had recommended that provision be made for
officers occupying certain positions "to advance
through two or even three classes irrespective of the
occurrence of vacancies and without formal reclassification of office."[10]   Since the war the Board has
partially adopted this principle by attaching to some
positions, especially those at the more senior levels,
relatively broad salary scales.   On the whole, however, the system remains a rigid one.

RECRUITMENT[11]

One of the most distinguishing features of the
Commonwealth Public Service has been the tight
control exercised over the entrance channels.   Both
the 1902 and 1922 Public Service Acts carefully
defined the methods of recruitment, and entrusted
their administration exclusively to the Public Service
Commissioners.

I. EXAMINATIONS

Direct Examination.   The standard method of
recruitment to the Clerical or Third Division, and

[9] Canberra Research Group, "Commonwealth Policy Co-
ordination," *Public Administration*, Dec., 1955, p. 208.

[10] *Royal Commission Report*, p. 43.

[11] Much of the material relating to the early examination
system which has been included in this section is based on a
detailed survey compiled by the Research Section of the Public
Service Board.

therefore to the higher administrative offices, has
been by examination of youths from outside the
Service. During the operation of the 1902 Act
these entrance examinations were held on a statewide
basis at irregular intervals determined by the needs
of the departments within each state. By regulations
the Commissioner prescribed the subjects in which
each clerical candidate was to be examined. These
included handwriting, spelling, English (including
essay writing, correction of grammatical errors, analysis and meaning of words), arithmetic, geography,
and English history. In addition the candidate could
be examined in any two optional subjects: mathe-
matics, Latin, French, German, and physics.[12]   In
1907 an examination in shorthand and typing was
added to the list of optionals. The candidate was not
compelled to attempt any more than the compulsory
subjects, but by earning additional marks in the
optional subjects he could improve his chances of
selection from the list of eligibles. Appointments
were made in order of merit.

Considering that at the beginning of the century
there were only a few state-supported secondary
schools in Australia,[13] the standard of the clerical
examination appears to have been reasonably sound.
Although it is impossible to attempt exact com-

[12] Public Service Commissioner, *First Report* (1904), p. 19.
Examinations for appointment to the Professional Division, which
were limited in number, stressed more technical subjects.

[13] In Victoria, Tasmania, and Western Australia there were
none. By 1910 the number of pupils in secondary schools was
approximately six thousand. See Parker, pp. 84-85.

parisons, it has been estimated that the standard of the compulsory subjects was at least equal to the present Melbourne University Intermediate Certificate, while the optional subjects approximated the present Leaving Certificate standard.[14]

The procedure and syllabus of the clerical entrance examination remained substantially unchanged until 1917. The Commissioner then reported that because of the lack of sufficient successful candidates it had been decided to accept as eligible for appointment those who had passed the Intermediate Certificate Examination of New South Wales or the Junior Public Examination of Queensland. In his opinion, a factor militating against success in the clerical examination had been the failure to integrate the prescribed subjects with the usual school curriculum.[15] Six examinations of this type were held over the three-year period 1917-1919.

Another procedural modification introduced during the same period was a series of special examinations conducted at sub-Intermediate Certificate level and restricted to returned soldiers. Compulsory subjects were limited to handwriting, dictation, English, and arithmetic, the standard of

[14] In Australia the Intermediate or Junior Examination is given to youths after they complete a secondary-education course which normally requires three years. The Leaving or Senior Examination is based on an additional one or two years study. Although it is impossible to draw exact comparisons, the two examinations are given to students who are approximately the ages of graduates of American junior high schools and senior high schools, respectively.

[15] Public Service Commissioner, *Thirteenth Report* (1918), pp. 15-16.

the latter two subjects being lower than in the regular clerical examination. The subjects of bookkeeping and business knowledge, and elementary chemistry —both at a standard below Intermediate level—were added to the list of acceptable optional subjects. Indicative of the lowered standard of these examinations is the fact that the number of those successful approached 75 per cent of the total candidates, whereas the normal figure had been 33 per cent.[16]

An examination conducted in November, 1918, was the last of the regular series of clerical examinations to be administered by the Public Service Commissioner, for during most of the twenties appointment to the Third Division was the exclusive privilege of returned soldiers. In consequence of the absolute preference clause incorporated into the 1922 Public Service Act and the large number of returned soldiers who had qualified for appointment through one of the modified examinations or who were able to qualify through other public examinations (see below), it was futile for the Board to continue to conduct public examinations. It was not until 1927 that another clerical examination was held (for appointment in Canberra), followed by one in 1928, two in 1930, and one in 1933. In all, from 1918 to 1932 only forty-nine appointments to the Third Division were made through examination.[17]

In 1935 the Board introduced the practice of

[16] Public Service Commissioner, *Seventeenth Report* (1922), p. 11.
[17] Public Service Board, *Twenty-Fourth Report* (1948), p. 13.

conducting its appointment examination in conjunction with the Leaving Certificate Examination administered by the state educational authorities, and the
great majority of entrants to the Third Division now
qualify by this means. The Board requires a pass
on four subjects, including English.[18]

Transfer Examination. The next largest source
of recruits to the Third Division has been by transfer
from the General or Fourth Division by means of
examination. During the period covered by the 1902
Act these examinations were usually held in conjunction with the outside appointment examinations
already referred to, although examinations were conducted in some instances exclusively for outsiders,
and in others exclusively for insiders. Under provisions of the Act it was necessary for an officer of
the General Division to have been in the Service for
at least two years before being eligible for candidacy,
and Section 23 (4) stipulated that the standard of
the transfer examination was to be the same as that
for admission to the Clerical Division by direct appointment. Thus there was no question of compro-
mising the standard of entrance. However, when
transfer examinations were held in conjunction with
appointment examinations, selection was not always
in order of merit. Many times a larger proportion
of vacancies was declared open for insiders than for
outsiders.

[18] In addition to English the subjects usually chosen include
British history, Australian history, geography, arithmetic, algebra,
geometry, commercial law, accounting, and economics and
government administration.

Transfer examinations were held at irregular intervals from 1903 to 1918.[19] From 1919 to 1922 only officers of the General Division with veteran status were eligible to sit for the examination; and from 1922 to 1927 the examinations were suspended altogether. During the period 1927-1933 seven examinations were conducted for Fourth Division officers, four being in conjunction with appointment examinations. Finally, in 1935 the Board instituted the present practice of conducting what is referred to as the annual "clerical examination," an examination designed for officers of the Fourth Division in all states to qualify for transfer to the Third Division.

Unlike the original legislation, the 1922 Act contained no provision requiring that the standards of the transfer and entrance examinations be equal. And although it is usually alleged that equality has been maintained, certain concessions have, in fact, been given to insiders who seek transfer to the Third Division. One observer, therefore, writing in 1941, concluded that the transfer examination opened a "back door" entry into the higher ranks of the Service, a judgment which was reinforced by the Board's policy of appointing eligible candidates from the transfer examination in numbers equal to those qualifying at the Leaving Certificate examination.[20]

Transfer from the Fourth Division is usually

[19] In all, from 1903 to 1918 the number of appointments made to the Clerical Division from the transfer examination (1199) about equaled the number made from the outside examination (1364).

[20] Parker, pp. 176-177.

to a base-grade clerical position in any department. Provision does exist, however, for transfer to certain specialist offices in the departments of Postmaster-General, Customs and Excise, and Civil Aviation by specialized examinations designed for Fourth Division officers of these Departments. Major stress is placed upon technical proficiency, and the educational standard is lower than that of the normal transfer examination.

Returned Soldier Recruitment. Partly as a result of pressure upon the Government by returned soldiers' organizations and partly as a manifestation of Australia's rather tenacious pride in its ANZACs, veteran appointment has been a cardinal feature of Commonwealth recruitment policy. Although the Public Service Board has displayed continued awareness of the possible dangers associated with this method of recruitment, for many years it was powerless against political forces favoring such a cause.[21]

The first concession to returned soldiers resulted from legislation enacted in 1915 granting preference for appointment to veterans who passed the clerical examination. That is, for returned soldiers the examination was made a qualifying, not a competitive, one. Age and health qualifications were also relaxed. Two years later legislation was enacted empowering the Commissioner to hold examinations to the Cleri-

[21] For typical statements of the Public Service Commissioner and Public Service Board regarding the dangers of veteran recruitment, see Public Service Commissioner, *Sixteenth Report* (1921), pp. 14-15; *Seventeenth Report* (1922), pp. 10-11; Public Service Board, *Fifth Report* (1928), p. 17.

cal Division confined exclusively to returned soldiers and, as has been mentioned, based on an educational standard lower than the normal entrance requirements. More important, the 1917 Act authorized the Commissioner to prescribe by regulation a list of substitute examinations which could be offered by returned soldiers as qualification for appointment to the Clerical Division. The lowest acceptable standard corresponded with the reduced standard of the special returned soldier examination conducted by the Commissioner, and veteran preference was absolute. In retrospect, the 1917 legislation, which was introduced by the Government of the colorful Billy Hughes, appears to have been one of the less constructive achievements of that administration. While normal youth recruitment between 1918 and 1932 was limited to a total of 49 appointments, veteran appointments numbered 1,031.

Veterans who qualify by the Intermediate Certificate, or by passing any of an extensive list of public examinations enumerated in the regulations, still constitute a significant portion of the annual intake into the Third Division. However, as explained in a later chapter, preference is no longer absolute.

II. OTHER METHODS OF APPOINTMENT

University Graduate Recruitment. In 1933 Section 36A was added to the Public Service Act. This amendment authorized, under certain restrictions, the appointment to the Service of university graduates. The restrictive provisions required (1) that the graduate be from an Australian university and be not more than twenty-five years of age; (2) that he be appointed to a base-grade position in the Third Division at a commencing salary prescribed by the Board; and (3) that the number of graduates each year not exceed 10 per cent of the positions proposed to be filled by the Board through normal methods, i.e., the Leaving Certificate examination.

The passage of Section 36A marked the culmination of a series of discussions commencing in 1925 between various university organizations, the Public Service Board, and the Government. In general, the argument submitted by these university groups was that there existed many "weak spots" in the administrative staffs of Commonwealth departments, and that these were due largely "to lack of an adequate education on the part of officers who have risen to important positions."[22] The report of the British Economic Mission in 1929 not only endorsed this view, doubting "whether the system followed in Australia sets out to attract the best available talent to the Civil Services," but also suggested that Australia model its public services more upon the British example and establish a distinct administrative grade.[23]

Because the turnover in the personnel of the Public Service Board assumed significant proportions during the period 1925-1933, it is not surprising that

[22] Letter to Commonwealth Public Service Board of Commissioners from Standing Advisory Committee of the Australian Universities, University of Melbourne, Aug. 26, 1927.
[23] British Economic Mission, *Report* (Canberra, 1929), p. 40.

the Board's attitude in response to these representations appears to have been rather inconsistent. Initially, the Board defended its recruitment policies by pointing out that several graduate engineers had recently been recruited into the Postmaster-General's Department (appointed under Section 47 of the Public Service Act[24]) and drew attention to the fact that promotion to certain professional positions depended upon the possession of university qualifications. The Board also stressed its inability to flout the provisions of the Public Service Act in relation to veterans' preference; and later it pleaded that the retrenchment brought about by the depression rendered impractical the commencement of a program which would have had the effect of seriously restricting the already limited advancement opportunities for Fourth Division officers.

In 1929 the attitude of the Board, publicly at least, appeared more favorable. According to its report issued in that year:

The Board has always appreciated the increased efficiency which would ultimately result from inclusion in the Service of a leaven of highly educated recruits who have continued their educational studies to the stage of graduating at a University and are therefore beyond the usual entrance age for junior clerks. . . . The strengthening of the Service by the appointment of a restricted number of University graduates from time to time will assist in building up a reserve for filling the higher departmental positions, without interfering with the ad-

[24] See below.

vancement of officers within the Service who may demonstrate their fitness to undertake the high responsibilities of
office.[25]

Rather than representing the expression of a positive
conviction that graduate recruitment should be a
cardinal feature of policy, such official concessions
to higher education seem to have been prompted
largely by the realization that the heavy influx of
returned soldiers and the cessation of youth recruitment during the twenties had seriously weakened the
Service. This conclusion is suggested by the reference made by the Board, in the 1929 report and in
several previous ones, to the dire results of the
abandonment of youth recruitment and the increasing
difficulty in filling vacancies in the higher ranks of
the Service. The phrase "from time to time" further
suggests the equivocal nature of the Board's position.

By 1933 the recruitment of junior clerks had
been resumed, and preparations were being made for
the commencement of regular annual recruitment
programs similar to those which had been conducted
by the Public Service Commissioner prior to 1918.
At this time, then, the Board, while recognizing that
"under certain conditions some benefit might accrue
to the Service by the appointment of graduates," was
"doubtful whether the inducement that could be
offered would attract graduates who would eventual-
ly be of more value than the keen alert youth
educated up to the standard now required for entrance to the Service. . . ." Moreover, it pointed

[25] Public Service Board, *Sixth Report* (1929), p. 21.

out that since "the entrant must be placed upon junior work for training purposes . . . the conditions would hardly be regarded with favor by University-trained adults." The Board, perhaps having in mind the proposal of the Economic Mission, could see no op-opportunity "of establishing a distinct grade on the lines obtaining in the British Service." Indeed, in its opinion, there was "no comparable field in the Commonwealth Public Service for the absorption of graduates in positions akin to those of the junior administrative grades of the British Service. . . ."[26]

In accordance with the recommendation of the Board, therefore, graduate recruitment was to be regarded only as an "experiment." The Board stressed that it wished to avoid being bound to any long range and inelastic program, and that if graduate recruitment was to be introduced the Board should be allowed complete freedom in its administration. This insistence was in response to a proposal which had been submitted by the University Association of Canberra early in 1933. According to the proposal of this organization—the wording of which was in many ways identical with that subsequently embodied in Section 36A—the Board would have been *required*, "as nearly as practicable," to include in its appointments to the Third Division in any one year 10 per cent of university graduates. Curiously, therefore, the present 10 per cent clause in Section 36A appears to have

[26] *Appointment of University Graduates to the Commonwealth Public Service* (Cabinet Memorandum, July 8, 1933).

orginated with the Canberra group. Why the Board chose to retain the quota provision, rather than disregard it altogether, and chose to make 10 per cent the maximum limit of graduates which could be appointed in any one year is not entirely clear. Its own rather negative attitude plus the protests which emanated from the staff associations and their political representatives were evidently largely responsible.

In practice, the 10 per cent clause has not proved a hindrance to graduate recruitment. Prior to the war the number of applicants was not nearly sufficient to warrant appointment of the full quota, and in recent years the number of regular appointments has generally been large enough to allow the recruitment of as many graduates as the Board has been able to attract. Finally, since Section 36A specifies 10 per cent of the "positions" to be filled, not 10 per cent of the persons actually appointed, the greater the number of positions which the Board declares to be open the greater the number of graduates it is able to appoint.[27]

The greatest degree of latitude allowed to the Board by Section 36A was in relation to beginning salary. The principle underlying graduate recruitment was to be that appointees commence their serv-

[27] Thus for the year 1951-1952, 536 recruits were appointed by examination, while the number of graduates totaled 71, or 13.2 per cent of appointments by examination. See Public Service Board, *Twenty-Eighth Report* (1952), p. 21. Because of the expansion of the Service, the number of positions declared open by the Board has so far accurately reflected the number of vacancies.

ice career in the base-grade positions of the Third
Division and take their chances of promotion along
with other clerks recruited through normal channels.
In other words, the sole concessions granted to graduates by Section 36A were exemption from examination (graduates naturally held the Leaving Certificate) and a higher age limit.   But within the base
salary range the Board was empowered to appoint
graduates at any beginning salary it chose.   Until
1947 the minimum rates for graduates for each year
of age from twenty-one to twenty-four were identical
with those prescribed for Leaving Certificate entrants
on attaining those ages.   That is, beginning salary
took account only of age, not of advanced qualifications.   In 1948 the Board, in order to encourage graduate recruitment, raised the minimum rate to one increment below the maximum salary for the base-grade
range.   Thus a graduate recruited at the age of
twenty-one now starts on a salary three increments
above that received by the Leaving Certificate entrant
at the same age.

   Lateral Recruitment: (a) Outside appointments.
Section 47 of the present Act allows for the appointment "to a Division other than the Fourth Division"
of any person who is not otherwise eligible, providing
that the Board certifies that "in its opinion there is
no officer available in the Commonwealth Service
who is as capable of filling the position." A copy
of every recommendation must be laid before both
houses of Parliament.

The wording of Section 47 is almost identical with Section 31 of the 1902 Act. However, Section 31 applied only to appointments in the Administrative and Professional Divisions. The duties ascribed to the clerical classes were evidently seen as so elementary in nature that the framers of the Act could not envisage an occasion when it would be necessary or desirable to appoint to a "clerical" position persons from outside the Service with special qualifications or ability. But it is clear from McLachlan's report that such occasions did arise and that the provisions of the Act were circumvented through an extremely broad interpretation of the term "professional." Although acknowledging that these "professional" appointments had been justified and in the interests of the Service, McLachlan called attention to this obvious evasion of the spirit of the Act and recommended, as has been seen, that the Professional and Clerical Divisions be amalgamated and that outside appointments be permitted to each.[28]

Selection under Section 47 is always preceded by public advertisement and usually by competitive interviews conducted by the department. If the Board can be convinced that the selected applicant is needed and possesses the requisite qualifications,

[28] The restrictive provisions of Section 31 were not always so easily overcome. After World War I, for example, the Commissioner of Taxation complained that the majority of resignations in his department had been among temporary officers "who considered that, owing to the present form of the Public Service Act, it would be impossible for them to secure permanent appointment." *Seventh Annual Report of Commissioner of Taxation* (1921), p. 7.

and that there is no one available within the Service "as capable" of filling the vacant position, the appointment is approved.

Section 47 might be termed the Commonwealth's blunt instrument of recruitment. It is the substitute for a comprehensive system of examinations which would result from a logical extension of the principle of position classification, and it provides a convenient escape from a system of recruitment which demands that new entrants commence their service career at the bottom of the ladder and at an early age. Appointment under Section 47 is to a particular, and presumably specialized or professional, position; but once within the Service the appointee may seek promotion to any vacant position regardless of its nature.

Lateral Recruitment: (b) Transfer of state officers. One of the most important sources of recruits for the Commonwealth Service has been the state public services. Section 84 of the Constitution made provision for the transfer to the Commonwealth of state officers and assured the preservation of their accumulated rights; and Section 33 of the Public Service Act 1902 allowed the appointment to the Commonwealth Service of officers who, prior to federation, had joined a public service of one of the states. Most of the original staff of the Commonwealth departments were recruited under one of these provisions, while the Departments of Trade and Customs, Defence, and Postmaster-General were created simply by amalgamating the existing state establishments.

Section 33, however, applied only to officers who prior to federation had joined a state service. Presumably it was supposed that after the initial staffing of the Commonwealth had been completed, it no longer would be necessary to look to the state services for recruits. With the passage of the Lighthouse Act in 1913, the need arose to make provision for the appointment to the Commonwealth Service of lighthouse keepers who had joined a state service *after* federation. In 1913, therefore, the Public Service Act was amended to allow the transfer of state officers to the Commonwealth Service regardless of the date of their first appointment. Although prompted by this minor incident, the 1913 amendment, as incorporated into Section 44 of the 1922 Act, has been of considerable consequence. It has broadened the sources of recruitment for the Commonwealth, and for the states it has intensified the problem of competing with the federal government for skilled personnel.

III. CADETSHIPS

Diplomatic Cadets. The Diplomatic Cadet scheme, begun in 1943, represented the first attempt to provide a specialized recruitment and training program for nonprofessional officers. The establishment of a diplomatic service and the expansion of the External Affairs Department emphasized the necessity for a caliber of recruit not usually found among applicants from the annual Leaving Examination. Initially, the method of selection of diplomatic cadets consisted of a personal interview before state selection committees (made up of representatives from the Public Service Board, the state university, and a Commonwealth department) and competitive examination (modern language, essay and précis). However, because of the large number of applicants —fifteen hundred the first year—the selection procedure was altered to provide for a preliminary written examination, followed by personal interview of those achieving distinction. In 1948, by restricting applicants to university graduates, it was possible to dispense with the written examinations and to select applicants solely on the basis of the personal interview, first at the state level and then (for those recommended) in Canberra. About six candidates are now selected each year.

The course of training after selection has been altered in several respects since 1943. The twelve cadets selected under the first program underwent a nine-month course arranged by the University of Sydney. Beginning with the second group, the course was transferred to Canberra, lengthened to two years, and directed by a special School of Diplomatic Studies created at the Canberra University College, an affiliate of the University of Melbourne. In 1951, because the candidates were restricted to graduates, it was decided to modify the cadetship course and to compress it into one year. Finally, in 1954 the formal study course was discontinued in favor of individual courses when required and a system of job rotation within the department. In recognition of these many variations of the original scheme, the term "cadetship" was formally dropped in 1955, and the selected candidates are now appointed directly as External Affairs Officers, Grade 1.[29]

Other Cadetships. The Board has also introduced other cadet recruitment programs designed mainly to attract professional or technical staff. Cadets are usually recruited through the Leaving or transfer examination by passing in specified subjects, although some are recruited after entrance at a university. The selected officers undertake full-time studies at a university or technical college in training for a degree or diploma. They receive full salary, in addition to a refund of the whole or part of tuition fees, according to a fixed formula. During vacations they are required to work in the departments to which they are attached. Upon satisfactory completion of the course the officer is assured appointment at the appropriate minimum salary.

For many years the only cadetships available were those of cadet (engineer) in the Postmaster-General's Department, and prior to 1939 only four additional cadet schemes were operating. By 1955 the cadet system embraced fourteen categories of specialization, including diplomatic and personnel cadets. The latter, who enroll in more liberal uni-

[29] A full account of the early cadet schemes will be found in Department of External Affairs, *Current Notes on International Affairs* (1948), pp. 77-80.

versity subjects and also receive supervised training by the Public Service Board, are appointed personnel officers in their departments. There was a total of 475 cadets in training by June, 1955.

IV. THREE NOTES ON RECRUITMENT POLICY

Age Limits. The age limits prescribed for new entrants into the Service have been a logical outgrowth of the recruitment philosophy. New recruits are expected not only to make public service their chosen career, but also to make the choice sufficiently early to assure that their initial appointment as "clerk" will not seem patently inappropriate. From 1903 to 1909 the age limits for candidates sitting for the clerical examination were sixteen and twenty-one years. In 1910 the maximum was raised to twenty-two, and in 1915 to twenty-six. Regulations promulgated under the 1922 Act set the age limits for clerical candidates as sixteen to twenty-three, but when announcing an examination the Board can fix the limit at any point between these figures.[30] Returned soldiers have always been eligible for appointment up to the age of fifty-one, as have the special "outside" appointees.

With the exception of a brief period following the promulgation of the 1922 Act, there have never

[30] Because of the postwar shortage of applicants, the Board has relaxed its policy of recruiting only from the current year's group of Leaving Certificate candidates, and now accepts applications from holders of the Leaving Certificate on a continuous basis. The age limit for these "continuous Leaving" applicants is currently set at 28 years in most states.

been any age restrictions on candidates of the Fourth Division qualifying for transfer to the Third Division. Transfer to certain specified positions which require training is, however, restricted to those under twenty-six.

Employment of Women. Until 1949 women were not generally recruited into the Third Division. Beginning in 1903 candidates for the clerical examination were limited to males, and women were allowed to qualify only for transfer from the General Division. By 1915 even these examinations were restricted to male candidates, although two special examinations were then held by which women in the General Division could qualify for transfer to the Clerical Division as shorthand-typists. These appear to have been the last opportunities afforded to women to enter the Clerical Division until the inauguration of the new policy in 1949. Since then a significant proportion of the annual intake to the Third Division has been composed of women recruits. However, women still must resign on marriage.

Geographical Distribution. Until 1902 it was the custom to restrict appointments to the Clerical Division to successful candidates qualifying at the examination held in the state in which the vacancy occurred. In his 1908 report the Public Service Commissioner announced that "it would be more in consonance with the Federal spirit" if all successful candidates were made eligible for appointment in any state in the Commonwealth. For most subsequent examinations, then, this practice was followed;

and it has continued under the system of Leaving Certificate examinations.

PROMOTION

Because Australia has followed neither the British model of an Administrative Class nor the United States example of direct appointment from outside the service, the quality of its higher Public Service is determined to a large extent by the policies adopted in bringing through the ranks the officer who begins his career in a subordinate position. Thus in Australia the machinery governing promotion performs a role no less important than that regulating initial recruitment. It is not insignificant that the sole major inquiry into the Commonwealth Public Service since 1919—and the only major inquiry which has resulted in a thorough investigation by a representative group of interests—was the Bailey Committee investigation of 1944 into "Systems of Promotion and Temporary Transfers."[31]

Methods of Promotion. Methods of promotion may be classified broadly into three major categories: (1) promotion by competitive or qualifying examinations; (2) promotion from a list of eligibles restricted to officers possessing particular qualifications; and (3) promotion determined solely by the personal discretion of the promoting authority.

---

[31] See *Report of Committee of Inquiry into Systems of Promotion and Temporary Transfers* (1945). The committee was composed of representatives of the Public Service Board, employee associations, and certain departments. It was chaired by Professor K. H. Bailey, then Professor of Public Law at Melbourne University.

(1) In the Commonwealth Service promotion examinations are held only for Fourth Division positions.[32] During the operation of the 1902 Act nine examinations were held for Clerical Division officers to qualify for advancement beyond a certain salary figure within the Fifth Class clerical grade. The main object of the examinations was to achieve some measure of uniformity in the qualifications of officers who had been taken over from state public services. By 1910, however, the practice had ceased, and no attempt has been made since to examine Third Division officers for their capacity for advancement. In the opinion of the Bailey Committee, under the present classification scheme, and indeed "under any circumstances," examinations "could have only a limited place in determining fitness for promotion."[33] The committee, therefore, did not recommend their wider use.

(2) The 1922 Act empowered the Board to erect qualification barriers and prescribe conditions of minimum and maximum salary for selected positions. The qualification barriers governing promotion or transfer have been applied mostly to positions requiring scientific or technical qualifications, such as those of architect, engineer, medical officer, geologist, etc. Among positions requiring training of a more liberal character the following may be mentioned: Audit Inspector, Grade 1; Education Officer, Grade

[32] Apart from a few minor Third Division positions in certain departments.
[33] *Report of Committee of Inquiry*, p. 12.

1; Vocational Guidance Officer, Grades 1 and 2; and Research Officer, Grade 1. An officer cannot be promoted or transferred to one of these positions unless he possesses the required qualifications.

Regulations governing commencing salary and conditions of salary advancement *within* certain positions have been prescribed by both the Board and the Public Service Arbitrator. Although these, too, relate mostly to technical positions, they embrace the nontechnical positions of Assistant Research Officer and External Affairs Officer, Grade 1. The conditions governing these positions specify a fixed minimum salary which shall be paid if the occupant possesses certain qualifications and make that salary the maximum which shall be paid to the unqualified officer. Other regulations, such as those applying to various grades of taxation officers, lack the minimum salary clause and simply erect a salary barrier.

(3) With the exception of these positions which have been singled out by the Board, selection for promotion to any position in the Third or Second Division is determined solely by the discretion of the promoting authority.[34] The basis upon which selection is to be made, as spelled out in both the 1902

[34] The practice of selecting officers for promotion on the results of periodic rating reports has been adopted only in certain sections of the Postmaster-General's Department. The Bailey Committee, although recognizing the wide use of rating reports in public services throughout the world, was impressed by "the volume and severity of the criticism levelled against the system" and thus did not feel justified in recommending its general introduction. The committee stressed, however, that its negative conclusion was to be regarded as tentative. See *Report of Committee of Inquiry,* p. 14.

and 1922 Public Service Acts, is "relative efficiency" or, in the case of equal efficiency, "relative seniority." To date, the only challenge which has threatened the principle of promotion on merit was the legislation enacted in 1945 which, upon the recommendation of the Bailey Committee, provided for the promotion to certain minor manipulative positions in the Fourth Division of the most senior efficient officer.

The Public Service Act defines efficiency as meaning "special qualification and aptitude for the discharge of duties of the office to be filled, together with merit, diligence and good conduct." The Bailey Committee devoted considerable attention to the wording of this section, recognizing the criticisms which had been raised by the officers, on the one hand, and permanent heads, on the other. From the viewpoint of applicants for vacancies, it was contended that the Act discriminated against the officer who had demonstrated high efficiency and general capacity yet who, in relation to competing applicants, could claim little or no experience with the type of work to be performed in the vacant office. The committee, however, was of the opinion that the instruction memorandum defining efficiency which had been issued by the Public Service Board was sufficiently comprehensive in discounting experience as opposed to general capacity and aptitude.[35] Moreover, it refused to attempt to define by law a precise formula for determining efficiency.

[35] An extract from the Board's memorandum is reprinted in the committee's report. See pp. 9-10.

In contrast, the committee did recognize the need for a modification of the Act as applied to the duties of a permanent head in selecting officers for promotion to the higher executive posts in his department. In these cases, the committee reasoned, "the promoting authority ought to be able to make the selection with some regard for future contingencies as well as for immediate requirements." The committee recommended, therefore, that the permanent heads in making promotions "within a defined limited range of more senior posts" be allowed "and indeed required" to take into account qualifications of the applicant in relation to prospective vacancies in higher posts within the department.[36] Although legislation enacted in 1945 granted to the Board the power thus recommended, no action has yet been taken in defining the "range of more senior posts."

Promoting Authority. On of the most significant innovations resulting from the recommendations of the McLachlan report was the transfer from the central personnel authority to the permanent heads of the power over promotions. Under the legislation which had been in effect since 1902, the Public Service Commissioner, after a report from the permanent head, had recommended to the Governor-General the officer to be promoted. Under this system, McLachlan stated, excessive delays had occurred in filling vacant positions, and expense and inconvenience to departments had resulted. Moreover, the time of the Public Service Inspectors had been

[36] *Report of Committee of Inquiry*, p. 11.

largely absorbed in dealing with promotions and transfer, thus militating against their usefulness in other directions. In McLachlan's opinion, the heads of departments had come to acquire a clear conception of the principles which should govern the promotion of officers and therefore, subject to certain safeguards, should be entrusted with the promotion power.[37]

The far-reaching implications of the McLachlan recommendation were recognized by Parliament, and consequently a large proportion of the debate over the Public Service Act of 1922 centered upon its incorporation in the draft legislation. The House of Representatives proved particularly adamant in its objection and was able to force an amendment which returned to the Public Service Board authority over promotion and transfer. It was not until 1924 that the McLachlan recommendation was enacted into law.

Final responsibility for promotion, however, was not entrusted to the permanent heads. All promotions were to be provisional and subject to appeal to the Board. Under provisions of the 1902 Act an officer could make similar appeals to the Commissioner, but since the Commissioner himself, through the Governor-General, was the promoting authority and since promotions when published in the *Gazette* were final, not provisional, this privilege seems to have amounted to very little. With the passage of the 1924 amendment the review power of the

<hr>

[37] *Royal Commission Report*, pp. 26-27.

Board acquired added importance not only as a result of the new authority given to the permanent heads, but also from the practice of the newly constituted Board of gazetting all provisional promotions.

The Bailey Committee considered the question of whether permanent heads should assume final and complete responsibility for all promotions. It acknowledged and considered the arguments advanced for complete departmental control, but concluded that the drawbacks which would result from any change in the existing system would far outweigh any advantages which might be gained. The committee observed that to insist on departmental autonomy would cut directly across that section of the Public Service Act (Section 17) which imposes on the Board responsibility for exercising critical oversight of departmental activities, methods, and utilization of staff. Moreover, in the opinion of the committee, interdepartmental promotions implied the existence of an outside promotion authority, "at any rate at the reviewing stage," which can impartially determine the claims of officers throughout the Service. Finally, it was recognized that "strong staff dissatisfaction" would result from any attempt to abolish centralized review of provisional promotions. For these reasons the committee strongly recommended the retention of the system of divided control.[38]

Investigation by the committee, however, revealed that although most permanent heads were

[38] *Report of Committee of Inquiry*, p. 19.

satisfied with the working of the appeal machinery, a few, together with a large majority of the staff associations, were not. The associations alleged that the Public Service Inspectors investigating an appeal could easily allow their decision to be influenced by a hesitancy to challenge the judgment of an officer of higher official status, and in order to preserve harmony between the Board and the department concerned would be prone to support the department's decision. It was stressed that inquiry into an appeal was a judicial matter which should therefore be settled through judicial inquiry by a board or committee.

As a result of these representations the Bailey Committee recommended that the claims of appellants be heard before a three-man committee made up of one representative of the department, one from the appropriate staff association, and one—the chairman—from the Public Service Board. In cases where all appellants were located within a single state and the salary of the position did not exceed a certain level, the decision of the committee was to be final. In other cases the committee was to make a recommendation to the Board, which would have final authority.[39]

These recommendations were incorporated into legislation enacted in 1945, and promotion appeals

[39] This provision was inserted to prevent injustices from arising from varying standards of judgment adopted by committees in different states and to overcome difficulties in cases where the officers involved were of higher status than those on the committee. In fact, however, the committees' decisions are nearly always final.

committees were subsequently established in each
state and in Canberra. The legislation marked one of
the most fundamental innovations in Commonwealth
Public Service administration since 1922. Combined
with the present system of classification, distinguished
by short and overlapping salary ranges, the new
machinery offers wide opportunity to those who
would improve their rank. The number of provisional promotions challenged by appeal has averaged about three thousand each year, or 30 per cent
of the total. About 17 per cent of these appeals are
successful.[40] Perhaps more than any other feature
of the Service, the new appeals system reflects a political and social climate which places heavy emphasis
upon the rights and welfare of the employee. But
as already suggested, the costs in terms of unproduc-
tive man hours and organizational instability run
high.

Interdepartmental Promotions. The machinery
governing promotion largely determines whether a
public service becomes a government-wide career

[40] In 1954-1955 out of 586 successful appeals, 488 were
upheld for "equal efficiency combined with seniority," and 98
for "superior efficiency." See Public Service Board, *Thirty-First
Report* (1955), p. 26.

McLachlan considered the question of promotion appeals
boards and concluded: "The view cannot be expressed too strongly that the remission of appeals to a formal Board of Appeal
would involve a distinctly retrogressive step, and the retention
of the present system, with all its manifest defects, would be
preferable to the constitution of Boards of Appeal carrying no
responsibility as to the ultimate outcome of their recommendations.
The future administration of the Public Service is too important
and serious a matter to be prejudiced by endeavours to obtain
theoretical justice." *Royal Commission Report*, p. 48.

service or a series of semi-autonomous departmental services under the direction of a central personnel authority. The provisions of the 1902 Act were designed to favor promotion solely within the one department, the Commissioner being obliged to give priority for promotion to an officer in the department in which the vacancy occurred. In McLachlan's opinion this was a sound policy, it being obvious to him that in most circumstances officers trained in the department are likely to prove more satisfactory than those drawn from other parts of the Service.[41] He recognized, however, that promotion from other departments was sometimes desirable, and therefore recommended that interdepartmental promotion and transfer be approved by the Board upon a report from the permanent heads of the departments concerned. Presumably he did not believe that the opportunity for appeals would result in extensive interdepartmental mobility and had in mind only special instances where two permanent heads could agree that the promotion or transfer of an officer from one department to another was desirable.

The omission of the priority clause in the new Public Service Act together with the more effective appeal procedure did in fact open the way for greater extension of interdepartmental movement than apparently had been envisaged by McLachlan; and, as indicated above, once a provisional promotion is notified in the weekly *Gazette*, any officer, regardless of his department or location, may now appeal.

[41] *Royal Commission Report*, pp. 48-49.

Interdepartmental mobility may be encouraged by a department advertising its vacancies in the weekly *Gazette*. The department determines whether or not to advertise, and also may include in the advertisement the qualifications considered desirable. Of course these discretionary powers are conditioned by the appeals system. The Bailey Committee considered the suggestion by some permanent heads and staff associations that all vacancies, without exception, be advertised in the *Gazette*, but because of the delay which would result it rejected the proposal. The committee did, however, stress the value of interdepartmental promotions and contrasted the Commonwealth Service with the British Civil Service, which is "large, highly diversified, and long established."

The Appointment of Permanent Heads. The sole provisions contained in the 1902 Act relating to the staffing of the positions of permanent head were those outlining promotion procedures and those allowing for the appointment of outsiders to positions in the Administrative Division.

As has been seen, McLachlan recommended in his *Royal Commission Report* that the existing functions of the Commissioner in dealing with promotions be transferred to permanent heads and chief officers. He made an exception of First Division officers, however. Their promotion "should be made by the Governor-General on the recommendation of the Commissioner," and "where the Governor-General is unable to accept any such recommendation, the matter should be made the subject of a report to Parliament."[42] The former Commissioner made reference to an instance where an officer had been promoted to permanent head without the Commissioner's recommendation. Because, according to the old Act, a necessary precedent to the filling of any vacancy by promotion was a report from the permanent head of the department concerned, it had been decided "by legal authority" that in this instance the vacancy could be filled without reference to the Commissioner; there was no permanent head to make the report, and in the absence of one the Commissioner had no power to make a recommendation. Although McLachlan acknowledged that the appointment in question had been justified, he urged that the loophole be removed in the new legislation.

During the operation of the 1902 Act no person from outside the Service was appointed directly to the Service as permanent head. It is worth noting, however, that all such appointments would have been subject to the approval of the Commissioner, and were his recommendations not accepted the matter placed before Parliament.

Contrary to McLachlan's recommendation, the 1922 Public Service Act contained the provision that "Notwithstanding anything contained in this Act, appointments to any position of Permanent Head may be made by the Governor-General without reference to the Board."[43] The precise meaning of this

[42] *Royal Commission Report,* p. 50.
[43] Section 54 (2).

and other clauses dealing with First Division Appointments has never been clear, largely due to the seeming ambiguity of the term "appointments."[44] Nevertheless, the Act has been interpreted as allowing the Government full authority in staffing the positions of permanent head. The present status of the Board, now apparently more influential than in some previous periods, is suggested by the following excerpt from its 1948 report:

The appointment to vacancies of Permanent Heads of Departments is made by the Government, under the provisions of section 54 of the Commonwealth Public Service Act, and not by the Board. The bearing which such appointments would have on the efficiency of the Service is obvious, however, and the Government has approved the suggestion of the Board that it be given the opportunity of submitting its views before such appointments are made.[45]

POST-ENTRY TRAINING

The "free place" program, begun in 1928, marked the first attempt by the Public Service Board to provide post-entry training for officers of the Service. The scheme is designed to encourage officers to obtain advanced academic qualifications beyond the standard of secondary education required for entrance to the Service. A select number of officers are chosen

[44] According to the definition in other sections of the Act, the term "appointment" refers only to persons entering the Service from the outside. According to this definition, then, only appointments to—not promotions to—permanent head would be beyond the Board's authority.

[45] Public Service Board, *Twenty-Fourth Report* (1948), p. 6.

each year for free places at a university, the Board financing half the students' fees and the university remitting the remainder.[46]   Study by the officers selected must be done in their own time, i.e., in the evenings, although permission to attend lectures during hours of duty is granted when necessary.[47]   Beginning in 1953, the Board commenced to award about four full-time free places each year. Altogether, by 1955 there were 124 free place holders; and a total of 245 degrees or diplomas had been awarded since the scheme began.[48]

Since 1945 the Board has also awarded each year a limited number of overseas postgraduate scholarships.   These are given either to officers with outstanding academic qualifications who are working for a higher degree, normally of doctoral status, or to experienced officers who wish to improve their knowledge of certain specialist fields.

Post-entry training of a different sort is represented by an ambitious in-service training program commenced by the Public Service Board in the immediate postwar period.   Administered by a separate section of the Board's staff, the program is designed both to instruct selected groups of departmental officers in administrative methods and procedures and to encourage departments to undertake training pro-

[46] The University of Queensland has not agreed to waive half the fee requirement, but since 1954 the Board has paid the entire cost for study at this institution.

[47] It should be stressed that in Australia part-time university attendance is not unusual.

[48] Public Service Board, *Thirty-First Report* (1955), p. 16.

grams of their own. Originally the training courses were confined mainly to more junior officers, but they have since been expanded to include conferences and "workshops" for higher administrative officers, in which ministers, permanent heads, university faculty, and other speakers are invited to participate. Though it is perhaps too early to assess the results of these training activities, they do represent one of the more imaginative extensions of Public Service Board functions since 1945.

SALARIES

The system of public service arbitration has, on the whole, helped to keep the general wage level of public employment in line with the going wage of the community. With respect to the more responsible offices, however, it is generally agreed that remuneration has in the past been inadequate, and hardly sufficient to make the Public Service an attractive career.

In his *Royal Commission Report*, McLachlan stressed the desirability of increased salaries for permanent heads and higher administrative officers. He cited the examples of the secretaries of the Attorney-General's Department, the Treasury, and the Postmaster-General's Department, each of whom in 1916 were in receipt of salaries of one thousand pounds per annum. Moreover, he reported that out of twenty-three thousand positions in the Service only forty carried a salary in excess of five hundred pounds. Even the Royal Commission constituted to effect "economies" recommended increased salaries for administrative officers. It concluded that "The financial benefits which might be expected from the adoption of this policy, in its stimulating effect upon the rank and file, may be assumed to greatly outweigh the comparatively small amount involved in such payment."[49]

In McLachlan's opinion, a significant factor militating against increased salaries for the higher Public Service was the method of salary determination. He believed that the intention of the framers of the 1902 Public Service Act had been to grant the Commissioner full control over the salaries of officers of the Administrative Division. The wording of the Act, however, left the point in doubt, and, on the advice of the Attorney-General, McLachlan in 1904 had been forced to withdraw his recommendations relating to the salary classification of permanent heads and other officers of the Administrative Division. Later he recommended to Parliament that the Act be amended to give him undisputed control over this matter, but no action was taken. He summarized the consequences of political control over administrative salaries in his *Royal Commission Report*:

Under existing arrangements, advancement in salary of an administrative officer is practically dependent upon whether a Minister . . . decides to include provision for advancement in the departmental estimates, that this

[49] Royal Commission on Economies, *Suggestions Regarding Salaries of Administrative Officers* (1920), p. 4.

provision is permitted to remain undisturbed in the final draft of the estimates, and that it is endorsed by Parliament. . . . If . . . the Minister is prepared to withstand the attacks certain to be made upon him for recommending a highly paid officer for advancement, he is faced with the difficulty of convincing his colleagues in Cabinet and members of his party who know that no political gain— rather the reverse—will be obtained by promoting officers of high grade. . . .[50]

To correct this state of affairs, McLachlan recommended that all salaries of the First and Second Division be determined by the Commissioner, and suggested nine grades of salary to be prescribed by regulation. Like many other recommendations made by the former Commissioner, this suggestion was ignored, and the 1922 Act provided that salaries of First Division officers were to be determined by annual appropriation. Second Division salaries were, however, to be determined by the Board.

Since the war, the greatly strengthened financial position of the Commonwealth government has enabled it to offer more attractive salaries to its senior officials, especially in comparison to the states, whose resources are more limited. Also, the method of salary determination has been placed on a more satisfactory basis than before. The government has established a permanent cabinet committee which, in consultation with the Chairman of the Public Service Board, sets the salary of permanent heads, and thereby also the upper salary limit for other senior

[50] Royal Commission Report, p. 38.

officers. In the past, because of the necessity of maintaining appropriate relativity between the salaries of permanent heads and those of their subordinates, the Board was not always able to recommend adequate salaries even for non-First Division officers. In spite of salary increases, however, the Service has lost some of its most capable officers to other employment; and it remains generally true that in the Commonwealth Service, as in most civil services, the inequity between public and private employment is most apparent at the higher levels.

Finally, it is worth noting that the salaries paid to employees outside the jurisdiction of the Public Service Act have often been more attractive than those paid to regular "public servants." A list presented to Parliament in 1929 showing the twelve officers receiving the highest salaries included only two permanent public servants—the permanent head of the Post Office and the former Secretary of the Treasury, who was then acting as Financial Advisor to the High Commissioner in London.[51] In 1936, as an argument for higher Public Service salaries, the Public Service Board cited examples of trade commissioners and various officials of marketing boards who were receiving salaries significantly higher than those paid to departmental officers occupying positions of at least equal responsibility and importance. The Board notified the Government that departments were seriously disturbed over

[51] *Parliamentary Debates*, March 11, 1929; Vol. 120, p. 968.

the prospect of losing some of their most capable officers to these authorities.

Many of these anomalies have now been corrected, largely as a result of a government decision to allow the Public Service Board to approve certain conditions of employment in selected authorities formally outside its control. At the same time, legislation constituting additional independent bodies now usually provides that salaries and other conditions be approved by the Board.[52]

The discussion in this chapter has concentrated upon the machinery of Commonwealth Public Service administration, and has been presented to provide a background against which the development of the higher Public Service may be viewed. In Chapter IV it will be possible to see how the machinery has worked and to what effect. Further comments upon the administration of the Service will then be in order.

[52] Among the most important authorities outside the jurisdiction of the Public Service Board the following may be listed: Australian Broadcasting Commission; Australia National Airlines Commission; Commonwealth Bank; Joint Coal Board; Commonwealth Railways; Council for Scientific and Industrial Research; Overseas Telecommunications Commission; Aluminium Production Commission; Maritime Industry Commission; Stevedoring Industry Commission; and various marketing boards.

For at least the lower and middle wage brackets the determinations by the Public Service Arbitrator minimize competitive bidding for staff among Commonwealth authorities. An unusually informative discussion of this and other phases of public corporations in Australia will be found in Joint Committee of Public Accounts, *Twenty-First Report* (1955).

3

The Growth and Development of the Higher Public Service

THE EVOLUTION of public service legislation and practice has been paralleled by developments in the size, structure, and functions of the Public Service in general, and the higher ranks in particular. The nature and extent of these developments form the subject of the present chapter.

SIZE OF THE PUBLIC SERVICE

Departments. The number of Commonwealth departments provides a convenient index to the growth of the Public Service as well, incidentally, as a guide to the expansion of the central government. The initial administrative structure was formally created on January 1, 1901, and closely mirrored the intended constitutional limitation on the scope of federal activity. Four departments were established—the Attorney-General's, External Affairs, Home Affairs, and Treasury—and a fifth resulted from the transfer to the new Commonwealth of the colonial customs and excise departments.[1]

---

[1] In accordance with Section 69 of the Constitution.

Later in 1901 the post and telegraph services and the colonial defense departments were likewise brought under federal control.

By the beginning of 1939 a total of four new departments had been added to this modest establishment: Prime Minister's (1911), Health (1921), Commerce (1925), and Civil Aviation (1938). During the intervening years, the functions and titles of the departments had fluctuated considerably, new branches had been added, and a number of new departments had been formed only to disappear in a short time. Nevertheless, that the major business of Commonwealth administration could be encompassed within eleven ministerial departments as late as 1939 indicates the modest growth of the federal government up to that time, and also underscores the rather momentous changes unloosed by World War II.

Beginning with the war years and continuing through the postwar period, the number of departments more than doubled. Nearly all of the newly established departments represented outgrowths of smaller branches which had functioned prior to the war or, like Repatriation, had formerly been constituted as an independent commission. The major exceptions were the Departments of National Development and Labour and National Service. With the establishment of the Department of Trade in the early months of 1956, the total number of departments reached twenty-five.

COMMONWEALTH DEPARTMENTS

1901	1939	1956
1. Attorney-General's	1. Attorney-General's	1. Attorney-General's
2. External Affairs	2. External Affairs	2. External Affairs
3. Home Affairs	3. Interior	3. Interior
		4. Works
		5. Immigration
4. Treasury	4. Treasury	6. Treasury
		7. Social Services
5. Postmaster-General's	5. Postmaster-General's	8. Postmaster-General's
6. Trade and Customs	6. Trade and Customs	9. Customs and Excise
		10. Shipping and Transport
	7. Health	11. Health
	8. Commerce	12. Trade
		13. Primary Industry
7. Defence	9. Defence	14. Defence
		15. Air
		16. Army
		17. Navy
		18. Supply
		19. Defence Production
	10. Civil Aviation	20. Civil Aviation
	11. Prime Minister's	21. Prime Minister's
		22. Territories
		23. Repatriation
		24. National Development
		25. Labour and National Service

The Location of the Departments. When the transfer of departments from Melbourne to Canberra commenced in 1927, it was intended that relocation would continue in orderly fashion until the central office of each department was located in the capital city. However, the depression, the war, and shortages of material and labor have combined to retard the construction in Canberra of the necessary office space and housing accommodation, and in consequence over half of the departments are still located in Melbourne.[2]   The Public Service Board, and non-official observers as well, have often cited this separation as one of the most serious administrative problems confronting the Commonwealth government.   In contrast to the United Kingdom, for example, where the buildings housing the Foreign Office and Defence Ministry have actually been bridged, the Australian counterparts remain separated by a distance of four hundred miles.[3]

Employees.   The growth of Commonwealth administration can also be viewed in terms of the total number of public employees.   By June, 1939, the total staff (permanent, temporary, and exempt) employed under the Public Service Act numbered forty-seven thousand.[4]   This represented an increase of twenty thousand, or 74 per cent, since the basic

[2] The departments located in Canberra include Attorney-General's, Customs and Excise, External Affairs, Health, Immigration, Interior, Primary Industry, Prime Minister's, Territories, Trade, and Treasury.

The slow progress in the building program in Canberra is illustrated by the Administrative Block, still being constructed in 1955 although originally planned for 1930.   The history of Public Service transfers to Canberra is related in P. W. E. Curtin, "The Seat of Government," in H. L. White, ed., *Canberra: A Nation's Capital* (Canberra, 1954), pp. 66-80.

[3] See Canberra Research Group, "Commonwealth Policy Coordination," *Public Administration*, Dec., 1955, p. 194.

[4] Nonpermanent employees may be either "temporary," employed for a short period of time; or "exempt," for certain reasons exempted from the provisions of the Public Service Act. Most of the exempt class are manual workers.   Of the 150,500 staff in June, 1952, 73,100 were permanent, 21,800 temporary, and 55,600 exempt.

structure of the Service had been initially settled, i.e., approximately 1908.[5]

By June, 1952, total staff had reached 150,500, an increase of over 220 per cent during the thirteen-year period. The sharp increase reflected certain transfers to the Public Service Act of staff formerly under commission authority (e.g., Repatriation) or the state public services (e.g., income tax officers); increased activity of continued departmental functions; and the addition of largely new functions and services. The bulk of the 103,500 increase could be explained as follows:[6]

FUNCTIONS	
Post Office	37,100
Defence	15,700
Public Works and Housing	14,100
Civil Aviation	4,800
Immigration	4,000
Social Services	3,000
TRANSFERS	14,800
TOTAL	93,500

This rather startling growth of the Commonwealth Public Service in recent years has been the

[5] See P.W.E. Curtin, "Commonwealth-State Relations: Administration," *Public Administration*, June, 1953, p. 87.

[6] See *ibid.*, pp. 90-91; and Public Service Board, *Twenty-Ninth Report* (1953), pp. 12-13. The employment figures do not include 52,500 staff employed by bodies outside the jurisdiction of the Public Service Act. If these employees are included, the total increase of Commonwealth employees between 1939 and 1952 was 135,100, or 200 per cent. On a roughly comparable basis, the increase in United States Federal employment during this period was 183 per cent.

subject of widespread criticism, particularly by the
press and certain members of federal and state
parliaments. In part the charges have sprung from
the not uncommon conviction that "inefficiency" and
expansion are somehow related, but more often they
have been tied to the larger issue of Commonwealth
and state authority and to the argument that an
increase in federal employees reflects an intrusion into
state responsibilities or an overlapping of federal and
state functions. As the above figures illustrate, however, the sharp increases in the number of federal
employees have occurred in the fields which are
undoubtedly the responsibility of the federal government. Thus, regardless of what overlapping there
may be, its elimination would seemingly put only
a small dent in total employment figures. When
in 1951 the Commonwealth and state Public Service
Commissioners met to discuss the question of overlapping of functions, it is reported that the discussion
centered on the Department of Labour and National
Service and the Commonwealth Office of Education,
which together employed less than two thousand
staff.[7]

Two features of the enlarged Public Service may
be noted. First, the Service is now more fully representative of diverse types of employment and is no
longer dominated by a single department. Whereas
in 1939 the Postmaster-General's Department comprised 75 per cent of the total Service, by 1952 the
figure had dropped to 48 per cent. The other

[7] Curtin, pp. 89-90.

important implication to be drawn from the increased number of Commonwealth employees is that the Public Service, now comprising a significant portion of the working population, has become an instrument of economic policy. Thus in 1951 the Menzies Government directed the Public Service Board to reduce the Service by eighty-five hundred in order to relieve inflationary pressure and to direct the nation's manpower resources to their most productive use.

STRUCTURE OF THE HIGHER PUBLIC SERVICE

1901-1939. Throughout the history of the Commonwealth Service the office of permanent head has been the highest to which public servants could aspire. Inherited from the colonial services, the office has assured succeeding Governments stability and continuity of administration and has been a source of strength to the Public Service itself. Most permanent heads carry the designation "Secretary" to the department; others, for example the Comptroller-General of Customs, retain distinctive titles. In a few instances, titles have been conferred by legislation, e.g., the Director-General of Social Services. Also, to comply with legislative provision, the Secretary of the Attorney-General's Department carries the additional title of Solicitor-General.

During the early years of federal administration the only acknowledged group of senior officers below the permanent heads comprised the administrators of certain departmental branches in the various states.

The large expanse of Australia demanded that there would be stationed in the state capitals responsible officials in charge of the affairs of their respective departments, and this contingency was recognized in the first Public Service Act, which authorized the Commissioner to nominate "Chief Officers," i.e., officials empowered to exercise certain powers in matters of personnel. Together with the permanent heads, the state directors were so designated. The Post Office and the Customs Departments were necessarily the most dispersed, and consequently the head offices attached to these departments, especially in the larger states of New South Wales, Victoria, and Queensland, were for many years the most responsible and highly classified posts in the Service, permanent heads excepted. Other departments also developed state branch offices, but until 1939 most of these were limited in size and importance. The major exceptions were the representatives in the larger states of the Attorney-General's Department, the Taxation Branch, and the Public Service Board.[8]

Within the central offices the permanent headships remained for many years the only senior posts. A chief clerk and an accountant were usually the secretary's immediate aides. Even the largest of the departments, the Post Office, began operations with only a permanent head and chief clerk, and not until

[8] In 1955 the distribution of the Service was as follows: Canberra, 4.8 per cent; New South Wales, 32.4 per cent; Victoria, 30.6 per cent; Queensland, 12.4 per cent; South Australia, 8.3 per cent; Western Australia, 5.9 per cent; Tasmania, 2.7 per cent; Northern Territory and overseas, 2.9 per cent.

the recommendation of the Royal Commission on the Post Office was a chief accountant appointed in 1910. Chief administrators were, however, placed in charge of certain essentially autonomous units within departments. In the case of the Director-General of Works (Department of Home Affairs), the office was created by the Public Service Commissioner, but more often the branch was established by an act of Parliament and headed by an officer whose title, divisional classification, and sometimes salary were stipulated by statute. These included, for example, the Commissioner of Patents (1903) and the Chief Electoral Officer (1906).

Gradually the higher echelons in the central offices expanded. The growth was often imperceptible, since an addition to the senior ranks frequently resulted from a reclassification of an existing office. In such cases the Public Service Commissioner or Board would assign a higher salary scale and usually a new title as well. Many of these changes occurred in 1926, when for example the second ranking office in the Interior Department—designated Chief Clerk since 1901—was altered to Assistant Secretary, and the post of Accountant in the Treasury Department changed to Assistant Secretary (Finance). In each instance the Public Service Board recognized that the administrative responsibilities assumed by these offices had antiquated their titles and remuneration.

Sometimes a separate post of assistant secretary was created *de novo*. The first of these was the Assistant Secretaryship of the Treasury, created in

1911. The administration of the invalid and old age pension legislation, recently enacted, had been assigned to the Treasury Department, and to the new office the permanent head delegated all his powers under these acts. Most of these offices, which had been designed to serve a particular function at the time, were redefined in later years, especially as changes in occupancy occurred. Thus in 1916, following a change in personnel, the Assistant Secretary of the Treasury came to devote his exclusive attention to matters more directly related to the major business of the department, while pension administration was delegated to a more junior office. And ten years later when a promotion to the assistant secretaryship elevated an officer who had been responsible for the administration of public loans, he carried to the position most of his previous duties. The only permanent functions assigned to senior offices have been those few which have been defined by statute. Thus, since the Tariff Act of 1921, the major function of one of the assistant comptrollers-general in the Customs Department has been the chairmanship of the Tariff Board.

That many of the "clerical" titles yielded to more realistic nomenclature in 1926 was partly the result of the Public Service reclassification conducted in that year and the application of the 1922 Public Service Act. The first Public Service Commissioner had shown some reluctance in abandoning the term "clerk," and could not be persuaded that second or third ranking officers merited classification in the Administrative Division. Rather, he tended to argue that the permanent heads, the chief officers in the states, and the heads of semi-autonomous branches should hold a virtual monopoly to classification in the Administrative Division and also to titles appropriate to that division. The new Public Service Board, while restricting the First Division to permanent heads, did allow a more liberal use of senior titles, and the new Second Division encouraged the concept of senior administrative officers below the rank of secretary. In addition to new salary scales, therefore, the 1926 reclassification resulted in a more general acceptance of the term "Assistant Secretary" (or, as the case may be, "Assistant Director-General," etc.) and a conscious effort to apply the title whenever a salary classification reached a certain level. Yet the Board was always careful to specify that what was involved was a particular office with specified duties, not a class of persons accorded a distinctive rank. Thus the complete designation of these positions usually included a parenthetical description, such as the Assistant Secretary (Finance) in the Treasury Department, the Assistant Secretary (Marketing) in the Commerce Department, or in several departments the Assistant Secretary (Administration). To a large extent, this practice is still followed.

In summary, the higher administrative structure in the central departmental offices which had evolved by 1939 was one which had resulted largely from a series of pragmatic decisions dictated by the needs of the moment. Division of labor among the senior staff was seldom clearly defined and was organized more according to individual competence and seniority than according to serious attempts to create a lasting higher administrative structure. Departments were small enough that informal arrangements were generally sufficient.

Since 1939. Several significant features distinguish the higher administrative structure which has emerged from wartime and postwar reorganizations. In terms of size, its growth has paralleled the increase in the number of departments and the expansion of public employment generally. The number of permanent heads has increased from eleven to twenty-four,[9] while the number of positions at the assistant secretary level, both in the central offices and in the state branch offices, has increased approximately five fold. To illustrate, new social service benefits have led to the substitution of a permanent head and five deputies and assistants in the central office of a separate Department of Social Services for a single Commissioner of Pensions and Maternity Allowances in the Treasury Department. Since, moreover, the federal government in Australia, unlike the United States government, assumes full responsibility for the administration of the social services for which it provides financial support, the directors at the operating level, stationed in the state capital cities, now occupy positions of major importance. Similar

[9] One secretary heads the Departments of Trade and Primary Industry.

examples which could be cited are Territories, Immigration, Works, and those other departments which before the war were branches headed by an assistant secretary or even chief clerk.

Together with the expansion of departments, organization based on the particular skills available among officers eligible for promotion has yielded to a more stable administrative establishment on the higher levels. An assistant secretary is now generally placed in charge of a particular division, and the responsibilities of the office remain relatively constant, irrespective of the occupant. This trend has resulted both from an increased volume of business, and from the need to develop greater specialization of function. Thus, before the war the Attorney-General's Department was loosely organized under the permanent head and two assistant secretaries, and these and other legally trained officers were available for any professional assignment. In contrast, a general reorganization in 1948 divided the department into three major functional divisions and two subdivisions; offices of assistant secretary, or equivalent, each requiring a particular *expertise*, were placed in charge of each unit. In the nonprofessional departments the trend toward greater specialization of function is likewise apparent, as the example of the Treasury, which has expanded from three to seven major divisions, clearly illustrates. In these and other sections of the Service increased specialization has been accompanied by the physical separation of major departmental components, a loss of the close official contacts which characterized the smaller organizations, and, incidentally, a narrowing of promotion channels.

Another feature of the growth of the higher administrative structure has been the appointment of assistant secretaries in charge of divisions devoted to internal administration. In the past the housekeeping functions normally constituted only a minor portion of the responsibilities assigned to a senior officer. Encouraged by the Public Service Board, even the smaller departments have now established separate administrative divisions to supervise personnel management, financial administration, and organization and methods. Faced with an expanding Service, the Board has found it necessary to delegate much of its responsibility to the departments and to encourage them, in turn, to delegate responsibility throughout their own organizations. The administrative assistant secretaries are, of course, officers of the department, rather than representatives of the Public Service Board.

Another position emphasized in postwar departmental organization, especially in the larger departments, has been that of deputy secretary or first assistant secretary. The posts are designed primarily to relieve the permanent head of detailed responsibilities, to supervise the directors of the various departmental branches, and to enable the occupant to gain an over-all knowledge of the work of the department. This trend has also been encouraged by the Board.

Finally, it should be noted that certain departments have developed series of positions of common designation which provide a balanced promotional ladder leading to the senior ranks. In the Treasury, for example, there are seven grades of finance officers, and in the Public Service Board four grades of inspector.

The changes in the structure of the higher Public Service are illustrated in the table following.

HIGHER ADMINISTRATIVE STRUCTURE IN THE CENTRAL OFFICES OF FOUR SELECTED DEPARTMENTS: 1939, 1952

SOCIAL SERVICES DEPARTMENT

1939	1952
Commissioner (Treasury)	Director-General
	Deputy D.-G.
	Benefits
	Asst. D.-G.
	Policy and Legislation
	Asst. D.-G.
	Finance
	Asst. D.-G.
	Rehabilitation
	Asst. D.-G.

ATTORNEY-GENERAL'S DEPARTMENT

1939	1952
Secretary and Parl. Draftsman	Secretary
Asst. Sec. and Asst. Parl. Draftsman	*Legal*
Second Asst. Sec.	First. Asst. Sec.
	Asst. Sec. (Advisings)
	Asst. Sec. (Executive)
	Drafting
	Parl. Draftsman
	Principal Asst. Parl. Draftsman
	Administrative
	Asst. Sec.

PRIME MINISTER'S DEPARTMENT

1939	1952
Secretary	Secretary
Asst. Sec.	Deputy Secretary
	Cabinet
	Asst. Sec.
	Deputy Asst. Secs. (3)
	Chief Economist
	Political and Constitutional
	Asst. Sec.
	Deputy Asst. Sec.
	General and Executive
	Asst. Sec.
	Sr. Executive Officer

TREASURY DEPARTMENT

1939	1952
Secretary	Secretary
Finance	Deputy Secretary
Asst. Sec.	*General Financial and*
Accountant	*Economic Policy*
Administration	First Asst. Sec.
Asst. Sec.	Chief Finance Officers (3)
Loans	*Budget and Accounting*
Loans Officer	First Asst. Sec.
	Chief Finance Officers (2)
	Banking, Trade and Industry
	First Asst. Sec.
	Chief Finance Officers (2)
	Social Services
	Asst. Sec.
	Chief Finance Officer
	Loans and General Services
	Asst. Sec.
	Chief Finance Officer
	Defence
	Asst. Sec.
	Chief Finance Officer
	Insurance and Capital Issues
	Commonwealth Actuary
	and Insurance Commissioner

FUNCTIONS OF THE HIGHER PUBLIC SERVICE

More significant than its expanding size and altered structure has been the changing nature of the responsibilities thrust upon the senior Public Service.

This in turn reflects new concepts of the proper role which the federal government should play, not only in relation to the states, but also in relation to the community generally. Domestically, the names of Keynes and Beveridge have come to symbolize policy objectives which no Government dares openly to challenge. The White Paper on Full Employment, issued by the Labour Government in 1945, clearly affirmed that the Commonwealth government was accepting responsibility for the maintenance of economic prosperity and stability, and that financial and economic policies were to be framed in the light of the objectives of full employment and a high level of national income. About the same time a new series of social service benefits was introduced to usher in an era of economic security for all. Full employment and security, finally, were but part of the broader goal of economic development of resources and an expanding economy.

External circumstances have likewise exercised a profound influence upon the role of the central government. Economically, the changing practices of international trade, together with the depletion of sterling and dollar reserves, have placed the government squarely in the center of the management of a dependent economy. And politically, the shock of near invasion in World War II and the subsequent revolutions which have enveloped Asia and the "Near North" have precipitated a national foreign policy supported by defense preparations.

In brief, government has become complex, and

thus administration also. The major stress of Treasury administration has shifted from accounting of expenditure to careful evaluation of budgetary policies upon the nation's economy; to traditional customs administration has been added the new dimension of import controls; free trade has yielded to the negotiation of bilateral trade agreements, bulk-purchase contracts, and international trade pacts; and for defense policy within the protective watch of the British Navy has been substituted military preparedness, which now consumes about one-fifth of annual federal government expenditure. These changes are cited not to minimize the significance of administration during the first forty years of Commonwealth history, but rather to emphasize the sort of administrative problems precipitated by recent events. The problems are ones whose solutions are to be found less in terms of executive or managerial efficiency than in expressions of thoughtful analysis and co-ordination. They require that many public officials become planners and advisors, rather than operating executives.

The first positive recognition that the Public Service could be entrusted with problems such as these was the suggestion by Prime Minister Bruce in 1929 that a Bureau of Economic Research be established in the Treasury. The Bureau was to study the economic implications of government policies. With a change in Government, however, the plan was allowed to lapse and, partly in consequence, during the depression years when ministries were searching for effective economic programs the Treasury was, for the most part, by-passed in favor of outside economic advice. A more concrete recognition of the advisory role of the public servant became apparent in 1932 when Dr. Roland Wilson (now the Treasury Secretary) was appointed to the new post of Economist in the Statistics Bureau. Within a short while Wilson's services were being utilized by the Treasurer and the Treasury Secretary to an extent not originally contemplated, with the result that his title was changed to Economic Advisor to the Treasury to reflect more accurately his major responsibilities.

During the same period there were other signs pointing to a new concept of the function of the public servant, as in the Customs and Commerce Departments, where the changing practices of international trade were reflected in the establishment of embryonic trade-policy sections. Nevertheless, such instances were few, so that by the outbreak of World War II the conclusion reported by the Haldane Committee on the Machinery of Government in 1918 might well have been pondered by Australians:

. . . in the sphere of civil government the duty of investigation and thought, as preliminary to action, might with great advantage be more definitely recognised. It appears to us that adequate provision has not been made in the past for the organised acquisition of facts and information, and for the systematic application of thought, as preliminary to the settlement of policy and its sub-sequent administration.[10]

During the war and postwar period new adminis-trative problems have led to the creation of a liberal number of divisions whose major responsibilities have been defined in terms of research, planning, and advising. Successive Labour Governments from 1941 to 1949 strongly encouraged the development of these units, and the Menzies-Fadden Coalition has shown no disposition to abandon them. Among the most patent examples is the new Department of National Development, which, freed from any significant executive role, exists primarily as a re-search and planning body in the fields of industrial and mineral development. Its activities, most of which were initially entrusted to the Ministry of Post-war Reconstruction (1942-1950), represent en-tirely new fields of federal responsibilities.

Other research and policy divisions have been incorporated directly into administrative departments. Of this development the Treasury affords a clear illustration. The Treasury began to assume effective control over economic policy in 1939, when the Financial and Economic Advisory Committee, a group of economists, was transferred to the Treasury from the wartime Department of Supply and De-velopment. Also in 1939 the first attempt was made to create within the Treasury permanent staff an organization capable of carrying out economic investi-

[10] United Kingdom Parliament, *Report of the Machinery of Government Committee* (1918), Cmd. 9230, p. 6.

gations. The Prime Minister and Treasurer, Mr. Menzies, supported by the Treasury Secretary, saw the urgent need for the creation of such an advisory unit, and although limited availability of suitable personnel forced a modification of the original plan, two positions of research officer were created. Finally in 1943, as part of the first major Treasury reorganization since 1901, a separate General Financial and Economic Policy Branch was formed. Thus for the first time the efforts of a group of permanent Treasury officials were directed primarily towards the formulation of economic policies, and this branch now constitutes one of the most influential units in Commonwealth administration.

The new emphasis upon co-ordinating machinery is perhaps most clearly reflected in the development of the Prime Minister's Department. Prior to the war this department had been little more than a congeries of unrelated administrative units, whose functions were hardly commensurate with the status of its minister. Since 1950, in contrast, the department has incorporated the major co-ordinating bodies which were created to meet the exigencies of the war and immediate postwar period, and it now shares with the Treasury the focal spot of Commonwealth administration. A cabinet secretariat has been organized to serve the full Cabinet as well as a new rationalized grouping of cabinet committees; and various policy divisions assure the department a major advisory and co-ordinating role.[11]

[11] For exceptionally candid accounts of these developments

Other prominent examples of the new emphasis upon "investigation and thought as preliminary to action" would include the Bureau of Agricultural Economics, an expanded Statistics Bureau, and the former trade-policy divisions of the Commerce and Customs Departments—since early 1956 amalgamated into a single Department of Trade. Indeed, it would be difficult to point to a department which has not, at least to some extent, formally recognized in its organization the legitimate role of investigation and policy planning.

The Public Service Board, in its first complete postwar report, summarized these developments as follows:

> Although the expansion in the scope of the Service has been striking, the transformation in the quality or type of function has perhaps been even more significant. Virtually every modern government has attempted to adopt a systematic policy to meet the fear of unemployment and the dislocation of the world economy through wars or depressions. Obviously, changes as important as these must have a profound effect on the Public Service under all of its important functions of advising on policy; interpreting policy; and giving effect to policy.[12]

The Foreign Service

Although the Balfour Declaration of 1926 definitely recognized the autonomy of each unit of

---

see Canberra Research Group, "Commonwealth Policy Co-ordination," *Public Administration*, Dec., 1955, pp. 193-213; and S. Encel, "Cabinet Machinery in Australia," *Public Administration*, June, 1956, pp. 93-115.
[12] Public Service Board, *Twenty-Third Report* (1947), p. 6.

the British Commonwealth with regard to the conduct of external affairs, until 1939 Australia's international position was, on the whole, one of colonial
dependence. Successive Governments relied upon
British naval strength, British foreign policy, and
British Foreign Office personnel to serve Australian
needs. Generally speaking, until the immediate
prewar years matters of foreign policy and international affairs aroused little public or official concern.

The evolution of Australia's international position
is clearly reflected in the history of the External
Affairs Department and in the development of overseas representation. Although one of the original
seven departments was titled "External Affairs,"
this designation referred mostly to such matters as
passports, naturalization, and immigration; and in
1917 the department was formally abolished as a
separate establishment. Not until 1935 was it again
constituted under a permanent secretary. However,
even by that date Australia, trailing behind Canada,
South Africa, and Eire, had not appointed its first
diplomatic representative. The High Commissioner
to London, appointed under the High Commissioner Act of 1909, and a liaison officer, attached
to the British Foreign Office since 1924, were the
sole representatives abroad. This picture changed
radically with the outbreak of World War II. Beginning with the appointment of a minister to Washington in 1939, the number of Australian overseas

missions had expanded to ten by the end of 1945, and to twenty-four a decade later.[13]

Meanwhile, largely under the aegis of Dr. Herbert Evatt, a new External Affairs Department was being formed. Following the establishment of the first legations, the Government decided that these missions would be included in the permanent establishment of the Department of External Affairs. Thus the alternate course of creating a separate foreign service was implicitly rejected. Simultaneously, the Public Service Board changed the designations of most External Affairs officers to those of counselor, and first, second, and third secretary. Salary scales were also adjusted. Thus at once the interchange of officers from Canberra to overseas posts was facilitated and, to encourage new recruits, a professional status was accorded to the departmental staff.

Officers designated by these titles constitute the diplomatic staff. It is they, together with clerical help, who staff the External Affairs Department in Canberra as well as Australia's overseas posts. They are public servants in the same sense as a Treasury officer, are recruited under the Public Service Act, and remain under the jurisdiction of the Public Service Board. They can apply for promotion or transfer to any department within the Service and likewise, at least in theory, any officer of the Service may apply for promotion or transfer to a diplomatic position. In practice, however, the diplomatic staff tends to

[13] Australia still relies primarily on British consulates, however. Australian consulates are to be found in only five cities.

comprise a distinct and exclusive section of the Service. This tendency, stemming in part from the specialized recruitment channels, is reinforced by a flexible allocation of departmental duties which tends to emphasize personal rank. A counselor, for example, retains his rank, regardless of the position he occupies either in the central office or overseas.

Although Parliament has enacted no legislation comparable to the High Commissioner Act or the Trade Commissioner Act to govern the appointment of heads of missions, in practice the same procedure is followed as outlined in these acts.[14] The Governor-General, that is, the Government of the day, selects the appointee. The Public Service Board has no control over the matter. When a career man is appointed, his name is transferred to the unattached list of the department, and he is given leave without pay from the Commonwealth Service.

Appointments to heads of missions are not necessarily made from the ranks of the diplomatic staff, however. Out of a total of fifty-three appointees commissioned between 1940 and the end of 1955, fourteen were politicians, eleven were military or civil public servants (Commonwealth and state), and six were taken from the universities or private employment. Nevertheless, as the department has become established, the trend has been unmistakably

[14] The High Commissioner Act is administered by the Prime Minister's Department, and officers attached to the London High Commissioner's Office are under the jurisdiction of that department. The Trade Commissioner Service is administered by the Department of Trade.

in the direction of the appointment of more career officers. Thus from mid-1952 to the end of 1955, eight of the eleven officers who for the first time were appointed heads of missions were taken from the diplomatic staff.

4

The Composition of the Higher Public Service

THE 1902 PUBLIC SERVICE ACT was based on the assumption of a closed bureaucracy with entry channels carefully defined and regulated. The Public Service was, on the whole, to be open only to youths who made it their career choice and who met the prescribed qualifications. The closed-service pattern followed British precedent, offered protection against the evils of patronage—not uncommon in the colonial services—and, at the same time, was in keeping with Australia's acute consciousness of the rights and welfare of the individual employee. Following the pattern set by the colonial services, however, the framers of the 1902 Act deliberately shunned the idea of a specially recruited corps of senior officials to staff the higher positions. Australia was an open society which was firmly based on an egalitarian ethic; and university attendance, and often secondary education, were luxuries beyond the means of many. Under these circumstances the British example was patently unacceptable and, in view of the functions of government envisaged in the early part of the century, probably seemed inappropriate as well. There appeared to be no compelling reason why the officer recruited as a telegraph messenger or beginning clerk might not someday make a suitable permanent secretary.[1]

An analysis of some of the characteristics of the officers who have occupied the senior positions in the Service will illustrate the extent to which the basic recruitment principles have been followed, as well as some of the resulting implications.[2]

[1] Australian critics usually look to London for the model of parliamentary government, and thus have frequently leveled strong censure of the Commonwealth and states for their failure to follow more closely the example of the British Civil Service in the recruitment of graduates. Seen in relation to other countries, however, Australia is not so exceptional as these critics would sometimes seem to suggest. Indeed, at almost precisely the same time, i.e., the mid-1930's, Australia, Canada, and the United States first began recruitment programs at the university level.

[2] It is impossible to define with precision those positions whose occupants should fairly be included under the designation "higher public servants," and any selected group is likely to be artificial and to contain its full share of anomalies. The officers who have been selected for inclusion in this study are those permanent employees, under the jurisdiction of the Public Service Act, who have appeared in the higher ranks of the departmental hierarchies (permanent heads, and other senior officers here arbitrarily designated "assistant secretaries") and whose functions include either advisory or major administrative responsibility. The selection has been guided by a bias in favor of the nontechnical departments and specifically (1) excludes (except for permanent heads) the Post Office, a commercial enterprise whose size alone merits it a separate study; (2) omits technical bureaus (Forestry, Meteorology, Astronomy), laboratories, and schools; and (3) confines officials in the Departments of Health, Works, Civil Aviation, and Defence Production to the top directors and assistants in the central offices, omitting chief medical officers, chief engineers, etc. In order to present con-

The Higher Public Service, 1901-1939

Recruitment Sources. (*a*) *Federation Appointments.* For many years the influence of the federation period was firmly stamped upon the composition of the higher Public Service. The first seven permanent heads were appointed by the Governor-General in 1901, most of them being taken from the state public services. By 1915 four were still in office; and one, who was perhaps the most distinguished, remained in charge of the Attorney-General's Department until 1932.

Exclusive of these initial appointments, moreover, twenty-two of the thirty-three officers appointed permanent head between 1901 and 1939 had been transferred from a state service to the Commonwealth Service at the time of federation.[3] As late as 1932, only two permanent heads had been appointed who had been recruited under the Commonwealth Public

clusions which may be representative of the Service as a continuous group of federal employees, three classes of officials have been excluded: (1) state directors of the Department of Trade and Customs appointed prior to 1920, a rough dividing date intended to minimize the carry-over influences of the respective state services; (2) officials appointed to the wartime departments but who resigned shortly after the termination of hostilities; and (3) those officials employed by departments or branches which, before 1939, were outside the jurisdiction of the Public Service Act (the most important being the Repatriation Department, War Service Homes Division, Northern Territory Branch, and Income Tax Branch).

Information on the particulars of each officer has been drawn from records of the Public Service Board and certain departments, the Public Service *Permanent Staff List*, the Commonwealth *Gazette*, newspapers, and the Australian *Who's Who*.

[3] Or in a few cases appointed by the Governor-General prior to the proclamation of the Public Service Act.

Service Act. A similarly high proportion of federation transfers was to be found among the other senior officials. Although the percentage of the former colonial officials in the higher ranks of the Service tended to decrease with the passing years, the last of their number to become head of a department retired as late as 1949.

In consequence of the large percentage of these transferred officers, the initial standard of Public Service recruitment—which, in view of the times, appears to have been fairly creditable—was reflected in the higher ranks to only a limited extent. What effect this limitation had upon the quality of the senior Service cannot be determined. It is clear from his early reports, however, that the first Commissioner found within the Service many officers who would not have qualified had they been compelled to submit to the entrance examination which he prescribed.

Recruitment Sources. (*b*) *Appointments under the Public Service Act.* Eleven of the permanent heads appointed between 1901 and 1939 were recruited under provisions of the Public Service Act. Six of these, who became heads of their departments between 1932 and 1939, had entered the Service by means of one of the regular Clerical Division examinations which the Commissioner conducted up to 1918. The other five, in contrast, had been recruited under one of the lateral appointment provisions. At the assistant secretary level, approximately 23 per cent of the officers were recruited through the Clerical Division examination, either directly or by transfer from the General Division; while 31 per cent were initially recruited above the base level. The recruitment sources of all senior officers appointed during the period 1901-1939 are shown in Table I.

TABLE I

RECRUITMENT SOURCES OF SENIOR OFFICERS, 1901-1939

RECRUITMENT SOURCE	PERMANENT HEADS*	ASSISTANT SECRETARIES
Federation..................	22(66.7%)	51(41.5%)
Examination Direct...................	6(18.2%)	$\left.\begin{array}{l}15\\14\end{array}\right\}$(23.6%)
Promotion...............	....	
Lateral Outside..................	5(15.1%)	$\left.\begin{array}{l}16\\23\end{array}\right\}$(31.7%)
From state..............	....	
Other†.....................	....	4(3.2%)
TOTAL.....................	33(100%)	123(100%)

*Exclusive of the seven original appointees.
†Recruited by the Defence Department. Prior to 1922 many officers of this department were outside the scope of the Public Service Act.

It is evident from these figures that during the period 1901-1939 less than half of the senior officers originally appointed under provisions of the Public Service Act were recruited through the regular examination channels. This can be explained, first, by the practice which developed, and still persists, of promoting professionally trained officers to senior administrative positions. It will be recalled that the outside appointment provision of the Public Service Act was intended to recruit this type of officer, one who could not be expected to begin his service at an early age and at a base-grade level; and later it was discovered that the same objectives of lateral entry could be served by transferring qualified state public servants to professional offices.[4] Thus the first head of the Health Department, an officer with medical qualifications, was initially recruited as a quarantine officer, and a new head of the Post Office, an engineer, was appointed to that post in 1924 directly from outside the Service. At the assistant secretary level, the laterally recruited officers included four surveyors (Directors of the Property and Survey Branch of the Interior Department), six lawyers (five being senior officials of the Attorney-General's Department), and five engineers or architects (four Directors of Public Works, and one Patents Commissioner). Well over half of these officers were initially recruited at the more junior level, and some appear to have completed their formal qualifications after entry into the Service either by attending a university or technical school, or by passing the necessary public examination, e.g., a state bar examination.[5]

Other nonexamination appointments, though fewer in number, can be explained as attempts to match the introduction of new types of functions

[4] See above p. 45 and p. 47.

[5] The use of professionally trained personnel in senior offices was also reflected in two appointments of permanent heads to the Post Office and Civil Aviation Departments, respectively, both officers having been trained in the engineering branch of the former department after initial recruitment at the base level.

with recruits of a caliber and with qualifications considerably above that which the normal entrance examination was designed to attract. The commencement of the liaison arrangement with the British Foreign Office following the 1923 Imperial Conference led to the appointment of three outsiders to the External Affairs Branch of the Prime Minister's Department; and later the first secretary of the new External Affairs Department was likewise drawn from outside the Service. Each of these officers was a university graduate. Again, when the Statistics Bureau turned its attention in the 1930's to economic analysis and investigation, two outsiders, both with graduate degrees, were appointed to newly created senior offices in that department.

The remaining nonexamination appointments were officers who were recruited laterally into all levels of the hierarchy as the Service expanded, usually following the addition of new administrative activities. For example, three officers were initially recruited from the New South Wales Service to occupy posts in the new Taxation Branch of the Treasury following the passage of the Land Tax Act of 1910 (the first Taxation Commissioner was a New South Welshman); and two others who subsequently became secretaries of the Prime Minister's Department were initially appointed to that department by Prime Minister Hughes during World War I. Some of these officers possessed formal qualifications, such as accountancy certificates, and one was a university graduate.

As a result of lateral appointments, the higher Public Service was drawn from a broader base than might have been anticipated from the design of the controlling legislation. Nor was it as closed a group as might have been expected, since approximately a third of the lateral recruits were appointed directly to the senior ranks without prior experience in the Commonwealth Service. It is clear, finally, that the qualifications of the lateral appointees added considerably to the average educational level of the senior personnel.

As already suggested, however, it was not unusual for an officer, once recruited into the Service, to study on his own time for some advanced qualification which he hoped would enhance his promotion opportunities. An accountancy certificate appears to have been the most coveted objective, this no doubt reflecting the major emphasis of administration prior to 1939. At least twenty-five of the senior officers considered who entered the Service at the time of federation or by examination subsequently qualified in accountancy; twelve appear to have graduated from a university through part-time study, half of these being law graduates in the Attorney-General's Department.[6]

Age Levels. Largely as a result of the different recruitment sources from which they were drawn, the age pattern of the senior officers showed little consistency. The highest age levels, based on the

[6] For six of the officers considered in this period precise information on their formal qualifications was not available.

age of appointment to senior office, were found among officers recruited at the time of federation, a fact which reflects the long period of time in which these officers continued to constitute a large portion of the higher ranks. Most of the younger officers, in contrast, came from the examination or lateral appointees, although within these groups age levels varied widely.[7] The distribution of age levels among the senior officers is shown in Table II.[8]

As Table II demonstrates, a majority of officers were at least forty-five when they reached the senior level, and not an insignificant proportion were fifty-five and over. This is hardly surprising with a recruitment system which generally requires that the officer begin his career at the bottom of the promotion ladder. Also, seniority appears to have exercised a rather heavy influence in promotion practice, as suggested by the fact that nearly thirty years after the first Public Service examination not one officer appointed by this method had become permanent head. However, had seniority been the only consideration in

[7] Thus, examination appointees became permanent heads at ages ranging from forty-one to fifty-one, and reached the assistant secretary level at thirty-two to fifty.

[8] Because the category of "assistant secretary" is necessarily an artificial one, and does not refer to the personal rank, it is impossible to make exact comparisions among different officers with respect to their ages when reaching these levels. Thus the figures in Tables II and V should be interpreted as approximate estimates which indicate certain trends. In some cases, moreover, the age of appointment to senior office could not be figured, as when an officer's position was reclassified to bring it within the range of positions singled out in this survey.

In Tables II, III, and V assistant secretaries who subsequently become permanent heads are usually listed under both headings.

TABLE II
Age at Appointment to Senior Office, 1901-1939

Age		PERMANENT HEADS			
	Feder-ation	Examination		Lat-eral	TOTAL
		Direct	Promo.		
60-	2	..	..	..	2(6.1%)
55-59	6	..	..	..	6(18.2%)
50-54	8	2	..	..	10(30.3%)
45-49	5	2	..	2	9(27.3%)
40-44	..	2	..	2	4(12.1%)
35-39	1	..	..	..	1(3.0%)
-34	..	..	..	1	1(3.0%)
					33(100%)

Age		ASSISTANT SECRETARIES				
	Feder-ation	Examination		Lat-eral	Other	TOTAL
		Direct	Promo.			
60-	4	..	..	3	..	7(6.0%)
55-59	13	..	..	4	1	18(15.4%)
50-54	11	1	4	8	..	24(20.5%)
45-49	17	4	2	8	..	31(26.5%)
40-44	2	6	5	6	3	22(18.8%)
35-39	1	2	1	6	..	10(8.5%)
-34	..	2	..	3	..	5(4.3%)
						117(100%)

promotion there would obviously not have been the wide range in age levels, at least among the examination appointees whose entering ages may be assumed to have been about equal. Perhaps only two safe generalizations can be made on this point. First, promotion policies seem to have been determined to a large extent by the individual department, some departments following a rather tight pattern of seniority and others being less rigidly structured. To illustrate, the average age at appointment for permanent heads in the Department of Trade and Customs was fifty-six, and for assistant secretaries fifty-two. In the Treasury Department, in contrast, the figures were fifty and forty-seven, respectively (excluding lateral appointments). Second, a rigid promotion pattern was bypassed in favor of more selective staffing at those points in the Service where new types of functions were introduced. Thus, the youngest senior officers in the Departments of Commerce and Trade and Customs were the assistant secretaries in charge of the marketing and trade sections. They were promoted to those posts in the early 1930's when marketing and trade problems began to assume new importance.

Mobility. As pointed out earlier, the wording and administration of the first Public Service Act were heavily weighted toward departmental autonomy. It was taken as axiomatic that the best candidates for promotion to a senior office were those who had spent at least a great majority of their careers in the department in which the vacancy occurred. During the period 1901-1939, 70.6 per cent of the appointments to permanent head involved officers who had spent at least three-fourths of their career in the department concerned; 58 per cent had spent their entire career in that department. Appointments at the assistant secretary level also tended to follow

a pattern of departmental autonomy.[9]   The relevant
figures are set forth in Table III.[10]

TABLE III
DEPARTMENTAL MOBILITY, 1901-1939

Percentage of Career in the Department	0%	1-25%	26-50%	51-75%	76-100%
Permanent Heads.......	4 (11.8%)	2 (5.9%)	0	4 (11.8%)	24 (70.6%)
Assistant Secretaries...	13 (10.6%)	6 (4.9%)	6 (4.9%)	7 (5.7%)	90 (73.8%)

THE HIGHER PUBLIC SERVICE, 1939-1952

On the eve of World War II, the Public Service
was woefully ill prepared to confront the problems
which lay immediately ahead.   In the first place, the
consequences of past recruitment policies had now
become fully apparent.   It will be recalled that from
1918 to 1932 a total of only forty-nine youths had
been recruited into the Third Division by examination.   The other recruits had been returned soldiers
who had entered the Service at substandard educa-

[9] In all, seven appointments to permanent head and four
to assistant secretary involved officers who had occupied senior
office in another department; four permanent heads were appointed with no previous experience in the department.

[10] In the case of branches breaking off to form new departments, the percentage of service includes the time spent in the
parent department as well as in the new department; and in
the case of certain functions being transferred between departments, it refers to the time spent in dealing with these functions.
Direct appointments to senior office from outside the Service are
not included.

tional levels or officers who had been transferred from the Fourth Division.[11] Even many of the latter were returned soldiers or officers of the Post Office who qualified by examination designed to test specific skills required by that department. To blacken the picture still further, the supply of veterans had finally exhausted itself just at a time when depression economies forced a curtailment of recruitment intake.

By 1939 these circumstances had combined to produce a Service which was based on a grossly unbalanced age structure, as well as one which had been denied those youths who, recruited to the Third Division at the normal standard of secondary education, were intended to provide the pool for the selection of future senior officials. As has been seen, not one of the veteran appointees had been elevated to a senior position up to 1939; and among the senior officers considered in this survey who were selected after that date, there were only five such appointees. This evidence would strongly suggest that the veteran recruits generally failed to compete successfully with the officers recruited through other procedures.

The account of wartime administration by the official war historian confirms the disastrous consequences which resulted from past Public Service

[11] From 1903 to 1918 entrants to the Clerical Division by direct examination numbered 1,364, and by transfer examination 1,199 (total, 2,563). From 1918 to 1932 the figures were 49 and 699, respectively, while returned soldier appointments numbered 1,031 (total, 1,779.). See Public Service Board, *Twenty-Fourth Report* (1948), p. 13.

recruitment policies. Referring to the few hundred public servants "who had both experience and capacity," he concludes, "One of the most remarkable achievements of wartime administration was surely the way in which so small a leaven worked on so large a lump."[12]

But the problem was more than one of a shortage of experienced personnel. There was also a virtual absence in the Service of officers who, by natural endowment, educational background, and experience were equipped to deal with the new types of functions which the Service was called upon to perform, ones which McLachlan and the framers of the 1922 Public Service Act could hardly have been expected to foresee. Economic controls, budget, monetary and fiscal management, effective utilization of the nation's resources, defense and foreign policies—these were functions which were at nearly complete variance with the type of activity which recruitment practice had been designed to serve.

Finally, beginning in 1939 and continuing throughout the postwar period, the Public Service commenced to expand at a rate which would increase its numbers threefold within a single decade.

The immediate wartime solution to the crisis in the Public Service was the temporary employment of as many outsiders—drawn from private enterprise, the professions, the universities, and the state public services—as could be induced to enter public em-

[12] Paul Hasluck, *The Government and the People, 1939-1941* (Canberra, 1952), p. 488.

ployment. And it was, on the whole, the noncareer
officials who carried the heaviest of the administrative responsibilities precipitated by the war emergency. Part of a more permanent answer to the
personnel problem was suggested by a special committee, chairmanned by an official of the Public Service Board, which recommended in 1945 that certain
of the wartime appointees be permanently appointed
to the Service. The committee apparently foresaw
that the war had set the pattern not only for the
volume but also for the nature of postwar government activity. In 1946, therefore, the lateral
recruitment provisions of the Public Service Act
were liberally applied to provide the Service with its
first major infusion of outside strength. Significantly,
many of the officers appointed at that time were
assigned to the Department of Post-war Reconstruction, a department which more than any other
epitomized the new administrative role of the federal
government. Other means of meeting the postwar
staffing problems included the appointment of additional outsiders and the accelerated promotion of
officers recruited in the 1930's.[13]

Recruitment Sources. Against this background
some of the characteristics of the senior officers
appointed between 1939 and mid-1952 may be
reviewed. Of the 37 permanent heads appointed

[13] Also during the postwar period there has been some ex-
change of officers between London and Canberra, perhaps the
most notable example being that of a British civil servant
who served for a while as permanent head of the Department
of National Development.

during this period (exclusive of the wartime departments) 16 were lateral appointees, of whom only 4 had been in the Commonwealth Service prior to 1939 (although 2 had been employed under other Commonwealth authorities). By mid-1952 13 of the 23 permanent heads had been recruited from this source. Below the level of permanent head, the influx of lateral recruits, although not proportionately as great, was nevertheless significant. They comprised 92, or approximately one-third, of the officers appointed at this range, of whom 68 had been taken into the Service in 1939 or later. The recruitment sources of senior officers appointed during the period 1939-1952 are presented in Table IV.

TABLE IV

RECRUITMENT SOURCES OF SENIOR OFFICERS,
1939-1952

	PERMANENT HEADS	ASSISTANT SECRETARIES
Examination Direct................... Promotion...............	$\left.\begin{array}{c}6\\8\end{array}\right\}$(37.8%)	$\left.\begin{array}{c}77\\63\end{array}\right\}$(50.4%)
Lateral Outside.................. From state..............	$\left.\begin{array}{c}9\\7\end{array}\right\}$(43.2%)	$\left.\begin{array}{c}62\\30\end{array}\right\}$(33.1%)
Graduates.................	1(2.7%)	13(4.7%)
Other.....................	6(16.2%)*	33(11.9%)†
TOTAL....................	37(100%)	278(100%)

*Two appointed at federation; four appointed to the Defence Department prior to 1922.
†Ten appointed at federation; eighteen appointed to the Defence Department prior to 1922; five were veteran appointments.

The new officials not only introduced into the higher ranks the benefits of their varied experiences and backgrounds; many of them, like some of their counterparts in an earlier period, also brought with them a new standard of educational attainment. In all, the lateral appointees accounted for 69 of the 116 university graduates represented among the senior officers considered. Many of the new appointees, moreover, had earned higher degrees or had been graduated with distinction or honors, an opportunity usually denied public servants who attend a university on a part-time basis. The picture in 1952 contrasted with that of 1939, when only 16 university degrees were represented in the higher ranks.

In the light of their background, then, it is significant that over half of the lateral recruits were concentrated precisely in those departments whose primary emphasis is upon functions which were in evidence to only a limited extent prior to the war and which now require a type of public servant that normal methods of recruitment were not designed to produce, i.e., the Departments of Treasury, National Development, Commerce and Agriculture, External Affairs, and the Prime Minister's Department. The same departments were also the ones which most noticeably brought forward those officers who, recruited at the bottom of the ladder, had attended a university part-time or had been recruited under the graduate program begun in the 1930's. Thus, of the 101 officers appointed to senior posts in these departments during the period under review, 68 were university graduates.[14]

Outside these departments the lateral appointees were most in evidence in those sections of the Service which had no administrative counterpart prior to the war (e.g., Labour and National Service), which proportionately had expanded most sharply (e.g., the defense departments), or which, as before the war, required professional or technically trained officers. Of course, the number of new officers shown would have been much higher had equal weight been given in this survey to the chief engineers, architects, scientists, doctors, and other high placed technical officers who staff certain departments. As in most public services throughout the world, postwar events have placed a new premium upon the services of the technical officer.

Age Levels. In view of past recruitment policies and the extent to which the Public Service expanded after 1939, it is perhaps surprising that more new appointees were not found in the higher ranks. With the exception of the lateral appointees and the graduate recruits, nearly all of the senior officers appointed between 1939 and 1952 had been recruited into the Service prior to 1920. This fact is directly reflected in the age of the examination appointees which, in contrast to the earlier period, averaged well over 50. The other recruitment sources provided the bulk of

[14] For the purpose of this analysis the Treasury does not include the Taxation Branch; nor does the Prime Minister's Department include the Audit Office or the Public Service Board.

the officers in the younger age groups, as is illustrated in Table V.[15]

TABLE V

AGE AT APPOINTMENT TO SENIOR OFFICE, 1939-1952

	PERMANENT HEADS					
	Examination		Lat-	Grad-		
Age	Direct	Promo.	eral	uate	Other	TOTAL
60-......	1	1	..	..	1*	3(8.1%)
55-59....	1	3	3	..	3†	10(27.0%)
50-54....	1	3	5	..	2‡	11(29.7%)
45-49....	2	1	4	..	...	7(18.9%)
40-44....	1	..	2	..	...	3(8.1%)
35-39....	..	..	1	..	...	1(2.7%)
-34....	..	..	1	1	...	2(5.4%)
						37(100%)

	ASSISTANT SECRETARIES					
	Examination		Lat-	Grad-		
Age	Direct	Promo.	eral	uate	Other	TOTAL
60-......	1	3	1	..	5*	10(3.8%)
55-59....	16	16	8	..	6§	46(17.5%)
50-54....	22	18	10	..	14¶	64(24.2%)
45-49....	25	8	14	..	3‡*	50(18.9%)
40-44....	1	4	26	1	...	32(12.1%)
35-39....	5	3	19	6	...	33(12.5%)
-34....	6	1	16	6	...	29(11.0%)
						264(100%)

*Appointed at federation. †One appointed at federation; two by the Defence Department. ‡Appointed by the Defence Department. §Two appointed at federation; four by the Defence Department. ¶Eleven appointed by the Defence Department; three were veterans. ‡One appointed by the Defence Department; two were veterans.

Some Consequences. One result of the recent transition period has been to make the composition

[15] See n. 8 above.

of the higher Public Service very uneven in nature. The imbalance is reflected not only in educational backgrounds and age levels, but also in general outlook. The varied career and social backgrounds of some of the newly appointed officers give them a point of view which contrasts rather sharply with that of officers who entered the Service as telegraph messengers or clerks in the early part of the century. The latter have tended to identify themselves with the whole Public Service "system," which, reflecting the Australian political and social climate, has traditionally placed heavy emphasis upon the welfare and rights of the individual officer; whereas the new officials have been attracted more by the prospects of meaningful participation in Australian maturization and growth than by the security provided by a permanent berth in the hierarchy. The opportunities for such participation, moreover, have given certain sections of the Service, particularly the key policy-making departments, a degree of prestige which was unknown in the prewar period and which still is lacking in the Service as a whole. These contrasts sometimes manifest themselves in ill-feeling engendered by selection of certain officers for promotion, in less than full co-operation between officers of departments, and in the decreasing influence of certain departments in favor of those with stronger personnel. In the latter connection, it is probably fair to assume that the failure of the Department of Trade and Customs to follow the lead of other strategic departments in strengthening its central staff with new recruits was at least partially responsible for the recent decision to strip the department of its trade-policy functions. Even the Public Service Board itself has been hard pressed to hold its own with other core departments.

Something of the spirit of this division within the Service can be gleaned from the vigorous protests made by the staff associations, especially during the period 1945-1950, against the appointment of outsiders and their subsequent selection for senior posts. The objections were voiced in numerous resolutions passed at association meetings, in petitions to the Prime Minister, and in frequent issues of association publications. Such protests from employee groups are not, in themselves, unusual and would be expected in any public service. What distinguishes the Australian situation is that the attacks seem to have been directed as much against the background of some of these officers as against their appointment. They are not only intruders, they are also, in the expression of one member of Parliament, "graduate goats."

A protest of a different sort came from the states. Noticing that some of their best officers were being attracted by the higher salaries offered by the Commonwealth, they accused the Commonwealth Government of "pirating" the state services.

In spite of these difficulties, the recent strengthening of the higher Public Service has constituted one of the most significant aspects of the postwar political scene. Professor K. C. Wheare, on a visit to his homeland in 1950, commented on the exceptionally high caliber of public servant which he found in Canberra and the "very great improvement in the quality of the Service since his last visit" in 1929. In his opinion, "the higher Civil Service of the Commonwealth will stand comparison with that of any other country in the British Commonwealth or outside."[16]

REPRESENTATIVE BUREAUCRACY

State Representation. One of the most important factors in determining the representative nature of a federal bureaucracy is the extent to which its officers are drawn from the respective states. It has been shown that where appointments are determined by political decision each state in the United States tends to be represented in numbers roughly proportional to its population.[17] In the Commonwealth Service, however, certain factors have combined to give one state, Victoria, a proportion of Commonwealth servants far in excess of the number its population warrants. The most obvious factor which has led to this result was the location of the federal capital in Melbourne from 1901 until 1927. Since, apart from the Post Office, departmental branches in each state were very limited in size, opportunities for

---

[16] Wheare also warned that if the Service continued to improve "with no corresponding progress in the States, Australian government will become a centralised bureaucracy. . . ." See "Twenty Years After: The Australian Political Scene," Institute of Public Affairs *Review*, June, 1950.

[17] See Arthur W. Macmahon and John D. Millett, *Federal Administrators: A Biographical Approach to the Problem of Departmental Management* (New York, 1939), pp. 292-294.

employment in the Service could be found mostly in Melbourne. The large distances which separated the capital cities usually rendered it impractical for one to move his home merely to reap the rewards of a clerical position. Moreover, the superior employment opportunities offered in some states (e.g., New South Wales and Queensland) resulted for a while in shortages of recruits, and vacancies in these states had to be filled by Victorians whom the Public Service Commissioner could persuade to leave home.[18]

During the early years of federation the higher Public Service was more geographically representative in character than in later periods. This was due both to the amalgamation of the colonial services in 1901 and to the appointments made at ministerial discretion prior to the proclamation of the Public Service Act. Of the first seven permanent heads, three were from the Victorian Service and natives of that state, three were from New South Wales, and one was from Queensland. In later years, however, the bias toward Victoria became more and more apparent, as illustrated in Table VI.[19] The increase in Victorian representation since 1939 is a reflection of the increased number of officials shown in this period who were recruited by examination.

In spite of the continued high proportion of

[18] See, for example, Public Service Commissioner, *Fourteenth Report* (1917), p. 6.

[19] Table VI includes only officers born or educated in Australia and for whom information was available. Where place of birth or primary education could not be determined, the state is taken as the place of examination or the state from which an officer was transferred or appointed to the Commonwealth Service.

TABLE VI
State Representation in the Higher Public Service

	NEW SOUTH WALES	VICTORIA	QUEENS-LAND	SOUTH AUSTRALIA	WESTERN AUSTRALIA	TASMANIA
1901-1939*	36 (23.2%)	76 (49.0%)	20 (12.9%)	7 (4.5%)	4 (2.6%)	12 (7.7%)
1939-1952	67 (23.2%)	162 (56.1%)	18 (6.2%)	17 (5.9%)	11 (3.8%)	14 (4.8%)

*The seven original permanent heads are included in the officers listed for 1901-1939.

The percentage total population (excluding territories) in each state is as follows:

	NEW SOUTH WALES	VICTORIA	QUEENS-LAND	SOUTH AUSTRALIA	WESTERN AUSTRALIA	TASMANIA
1901	35.9%	31.9%	13.2%	9.5%	4.9%	4.6%
1953	38.5%	27.3%	14.6%	8.9%	7.1%	3.6%

Victorians, New South Wales, the largest state, has at least come to be represented more adequately than before at the permanent head level. Whereas in 1939 only one New South Welshman was represented among the permanent heads, in 1952 there were nine. Meanwhile, the number of Victorians had increased from seven to twelve. Also it is worth mention that the representation of the non-Victorians has been due, to a large extent, to the nonexamination appointments. Thus seven of the nine New South Welshmen referred to above were lateral appointees; and of the fifteen Western Australians listed in Table VI only one was recruited by examination.

The proportion of Victorians in the higher Public Service will no doubt decrease as the older officials who entered the Service when the capital was located in Melbourne retire in favor of the younger officers who began their careers after 1927. Also, the growth of administration and the subsequent expansion of state branches will offer new opportunities for residents in the outer states. Appointment of university graduates, too, will tend to distribute recruits from each state university. Yet, as over half of the central officers are still to be found in Melbourne, and since Canberra, by Australian standards, is comparatively close to both Sydney and Melbourne, the New South Welshman and the Victorian, particularly the latter, will probably continue to be proportionately overrepresented in the Service. At the recent jubilee convention on Australian federalism, one of the contributors (himself a Western Australian) observed:

. . . the average Commonwealth Public Servant in an outer State suffers many disabilities. I sometimes think we need some kind of "Disabilities Commission" to study the actual incidence of disabilities among federal public servants! The system has a natural bias towards the man in the central States and this bias needs constant correction.[20]

Religion. There exists in Australia no problem comparable to that facing the Federal Civil Service of Canada in the employment of the French-Canadian, and the consequent political necessity to staff the

---

[20] P. W. E. Curtin in Geoffrey Sawer, ed., *Federalism: An Australian Jubilee Study* (Melbourne, 1952), p. 161.

Public Service with a proper proportion of a minority ethnic group.[21] The population of Australia is marked by its extreme racial homogeneity because of its isolation in the South Pacific, the White Australia Policy, and the encouragement offered to residents of the United Kingdom to immigrate. Only very recently have attempts been made to introduce the "new Australian" of non-British parentage. Within the population, however, there does exist a noticeable sectarian division along the lines of Catholic and non-Catholic which has its roots in Australian history and which finds most obvious expression in the composition of the Labour party and in the educational system.[22] The Catholic Church, and to a lesser extent the larger Protestant denominations as well, have established educational institutions at both the primary and secondary level, some of which are regarded as among the best in Australia.

The competitive employment opportunities for Catholics and non-Catholics in the Commonwealth Public Service have never been openly discussed, and reliable data are impossible to obtain. Nevertheless, several facts are worthy of mention. First, the Catholic Church has encouraged its youth to enter the public service, either Commonwealth or state, and through its schools it has sought to implement this

[21] See Taylor Cole, *The Canadian Bureaucracy: A Study of Canadian Civil Servants and Other Public Employees, 1939-1947* (Durham, N. C., 1949), chap. v.

[22] In the 1947 census, approximately 23 per cent of the persons who registered a religious affiliation listed "Catholic" or "Roman Catholic." Commonwealth of Australia, *Official Year Book*, No. 38 (1951), p. 554.

policy.[23] Second, the public servants themselves appear to be aware of discrimination which, it is alleged, is sometimes shown on religious grounds. This was recently made clear when, upon the protest of one public servant, the promotion appeals committees were instructed to ask no questions relating to the name of the school of the appellant or the appellee.[24] Finally, certain departments have acquired the reputation of being either predominantly Catholic or predominately non-Catholic and of governing their promotion policies accordingly. When a youth enters the Service he is sometimes discouraged by outside observers from entering the department of his choice because of the discrimination which, it is claimed, will be shown against him. The promotion appeals machinery does not appear to have mitigated this feeling of unfair treatment.

FUTURE COMPOSITION OF THE HIGHER PUBLIC SERVICE

Throughout its history the Commonwealth Public Service has relied heavily upon lateral recruitment to attract its most highly educated officers, originally in the professional and technical departments, in later years also in the core departments of government. Some comment upon this recruitment means, therefore, seems in order.

There is probably much more to be said in favor

[23] See Parker, p. 131.
[24] Section 116 of the Constitution provides that "no religious test shall be required as a qualification for any office or public trust under the Commonwealth."

of lateral recruitment than has ever been explicitly recognized in Australia. In view of the authority wielded by modern governments it would seem both necessary and wise that at least some of the senior administrators be drawn from sources other than a tight career service. Lateral recruitment can help produce a bureaucracy which is representative of the various occupational, geographical, and social groups of the community, and one in which the distinction between the behavior, thoughts, and expectations of officials and those of the citizenry is minimized.

Nevertheless, the disadvantages of excessive reliance upon outside appointments to meet the needs of the Service are apparent. Not only do they tend to destroy the concept of a career service, they also understandably lead to widespread discontent among career officers. The subsequent resignations of some of the recent lateral appointees, furthermore, suggest that they cannot be relied upon to provide the Service with continued and permanent strength.

Perhaps most important, however, the use of the lateral appointment provisions of the Public Service Act represents rather "back door" solution to the modern recruitment problem. The provisions were hardly intended to furnish the basic strength of the senior ranks, but rather to meet special requirements. Thus, an outsider can be appointed only if there is no officer available in the Service who is "as capable" of performing the functions required in the particular vacancy. During the war and postwar period there opened up an unprecedented number of vacancies which met this condition, particularly posts requiring some knowledge of economics (although in some cases the job descriptions appear to have been little more than thinly veiled biographies); and once past the rigid entry gates the appointed officers have had little difficulty in competing for promotion to the higher administrative positions. As far back as 1920 one critic observed that the defects of the Service recruitment policy would be more apparent "if the greater freedom of choice allowed for filling technical or professional positions did not furnish a means of introducing into the Service some men of education and proved talent who are then often put into responsible administrative posts."[25] Writing in a similar vein, a more recent critic, noting the number of senior officers with economic training, concludes that "economists (and, generally speaking, other experts) do *not* become senior officials because they know a lot about economics, but precisely because they are credited, or perceived, to have just those qualities of mind that are needed by an administrator."[26]

Public Service Recruitment in Perspective. To what extent, then, will present recruitment policies serve as a source for the selection of future senior officials who will compare favorably with most of those recently appointed from the outside? Stated

[25] Sir Harrison Moore in M. Atkinson, ed., *Australia: Economic and Political Studies* (1920), p. 89, as quoted in Crisp, *The Parliamentary Government of the Commonwealth of Australia* (New Haven, 1949), p. 238.

[26] S. Encel, "The Commonwealth Public Service and Outside Recruitment," *Public Administration*, March, 1955, p. 42.

another way, has recruitment policy kept abreast of political and economic trends, of the development of education in the community, and of the requirements of the Service?

The Public Service Acts of 1902 and 1922 were framed at a time when competition for employment was generally keen; when the educational system was at the stage when comparatively few youths continued school beyond the Intermediate or Leaving Certificate level; and when the nature of Commonwealth administration required the services of competent, but not highly educated, officers. Under these circumstances the chances that the Service would be able to meet its staffing requirements, in both quantity and caliber of recruit, were considerable. Moreover, it was very probable that among its recruits the Service would find at least a portion of the more able youths of the community, and that it did so is evidenced by the outstanding success of some of the senior officials who began their careers as telegraph messengers or base-grade clerks.

None of these conditions prevails any longer. An expanding economy and a positive policy of full employment have resulted in keen competition among employers for the available youth of the nation; and the effects of the fall in birth rate during the depression have recently been revealed in the small number of youths maturing each year. That orthodox recruitment measures have not been able to cope with these altered economic conditions is made clear from the postwar reports of the Public Service Board.

In spite of advertising campaigns, attempts to make the entrance requirements more flexible, and the holding of special examinations, the number of youths who have chosen a career in the Commonwealth Service has not been nearly sufficient to meet the requirements of an expanding Service and a Service in which, as a result of the recruitment policies of the twenties, the wastage each year is now considerable. In consequence, the quality of entrant into the Third Division since the war has been very much below that of the prewar recruit. Most of those who accept appointments are taken from the bottom of the appointment register; they have qualified but not competed.

One of the few bright spots in the postwar recruitment picture was the Government decision in 1945 to repeal the legislation which gave absolute veteran preference, and which was responsible for the disastrous policies of the twenties.[27] Yet so acute has the staff shortage been that returned-soldier appointments have outnumbered youth recruitment. In the period 1945-1948, for example, recruitment to the Third Division by direct appointment and transfer from the Fourth Division comprised 3,060

[27] Section 27 of the Re-establishment and Employment Act of 1945 requires all employers to give preference in employment to returned servicemen. There are listed, however, several factors which if present can allow an employer to hire a non-veteran, e.g., qualifications required for the position and "other relevant matters." Thus the Board (with the approval of the Government) can use its own judgment as to the proportion of veterans to recruit each year.

veterans and only 863 youths.[28] In its 1951 report
the Board admitted the dilemma it faced. "The
Board," it declared, "has hesitated to alter an entry
standard which, over the years, has produced good
results, but it cannot but be impressed by the fact
that if that standard had not been the Intermediate
Certificate for ex-servicemen the clerical services of
the departments in the larger capitals would by now
have suffered serious breakdown."[29] Not until 1951-
1952 did the number of youth appointments exceed
those of veterans. By 1954-1955 the ratio was three
to two.[30]

In addition to the low quality entrant into the
Third Division, the Board has reported that increasing numbers of Fourth Division officers are finding
it impossible to qualify at the annual clerical examination. This development, partly due to a lowered
entrance standard to the Fourth Division, has ac-
centuated the problem of finding sufficient Third
Division staff.

Some of the recruitment difficulties faced by
the Board will probably diminish as the effects of
the depression years lessen, as the age structure of
the Service becomes more balanced, and perhaps
as employment opportunities become less plentiful.
There are, however, two aspects of the recruitment
problem which will remain and which are reflections

[28] Public Service Board, *Twenty-Fourth Report* (1948),
p. 13.
[29] *Twenty-Seventh Report* (1951), p. 6.
[30] Of course, not all veterans are recruited at substandard
educational levels. Indeed, some rank among the most promis-
ing recruits.

of an expanding and maturing society. One of these relates to new educational opportunities. The Australian educational system has rapidly advanced to the stage where most capable youths not only recognize the value of a university degree, but also are able to afford the costs of higher education.[31] In consequence of the postwar inauguration of the Commonwealth scholarship scheme (under which university students are subsidized in accordance with the parent's income), financial problems will prevent educational advancement only in the rarest cases. It seems likely, therefore, that the more able youth, who formerly might be found among the recruits at the entrance examination, will now find his way to the university. As the Board itself recently stated: "... there is not enough intake of the right quality to fully ensure the efficient operation of the Public Service for the future. This is a situation which arises from a variety of causes, including intensive competition from other employers and greater opportunities given to youth of matriculation standard for university study."[32]

The other aspect of the recruitment problem is, of course, that the new functions undertaken by the most important Commonwealth departments demand

[31] In 1938 there were 12,100 students enrolled in Australian universities. By 1948 the number had reached 32,500; by 1953, 28,800. Figures taken from Commonwealth of Australia, *Official Year Book*, No. 33 (1940), p. 184; *ibid.*, No. 39 (1953), p. 220; and *ibid.*, No. 41 (1955), p. 420.

[32] Public Service Board, *Thirtieth Report* (1954), p. 5. The new educational opportunities also raise the question whether the free place program, which was begun in 1928, has not outlived its usefulness.

a new type of recruit which the entrance examination is not designed to produce; and the increasing range and complexity of activity affecting all departments demand more than the occasional officer of outstanding administrative ability which normal recruitment practices have yielded.[33]

For these reasons—the progress of the educational system and an expanded and more complex Service —it seems likely that the Service will be forced to look more and more to the universities to meet its recruitment needs.

The Place of the Graduate in the Service. To what extent, then, can the Service accommodate the university graduate? Perhaps the most startling transformation in the Commonwealth Service since the war has been the introduction of classes of positions requiring university degrees and the noticeably increasing tendency for vacancies to be advertised with the notification: "university degree desirable." One of the most significant aspects of this development has been the introduction of the position of research officer, which is now formally governed by regulation. Nearly every department includes in its establishment at least a few positions of this designation. Although the nature of the work performed many times bears little resemblance to what is commonly described as "research," the mere existence of these positions

[33] Another problem, which extends to initial recruitment as well as to promotion, stems from the location of the federal capital. The Board has difficulty persuading officers to move their homes to Canberra and to live in a city whose facilities are hardly equal to those of the larger urban areas. See Public Service Board, *Twenty-Third Report* (1947), pp. 17-18.

testifies to the need felt by the departments to employ officers with higher education. Furthermore, many departments have created positions peculiar to their own needs for which, according to departmental policy, only graduates with particular university qualifications are eligible.

The other aspect of this trend has been the very sharp increase in the number of officers in the Service who hold university degrees. In addition to the lateral appointees, the recruits appointed under Section 36A of the Act, and the officers enrolled under one of the cadet schemes, these graduates have come from three sources: (1) veterans of World War II who entered a university at the end of the war, assisted by the Commonwealth Reconstruction Training Program, and who were appointed to the Service under the veteran recruitment authorization; (2) officers of the Service who were veterans and who obtained leave of absence under the Reconstruction Training Program to enroll full time at a university or technical college (in 1949 there were 241 officers so enrolled); and (3) officers of the Service who completed a course of study on a part-time basis, either on their own initiative or assisted by a "free place."

From the very noticeable increase in the number of qualified positions and in the number of graduates, it must be concluded that the Service not only has accommodated, but also has come to place heavy reliance upon, the university graduate. But a question of equal significance concerns the nature of the academic qualifications required for these positions and the qualifications which are sought by the officers themselves. Is the Service designed to encourage the youth with a general university education, or are the opportunities more for the graduate trained in one of the special fields for which the Service has immediate use? Evidence suggests that the latter interpretation is the correct one.

What distinguishes most of the research officer positions and other qualified positions is their stress upon specialist qualifications, particularly qualifications in economics. In Australia the subject of economics has come to loom large among the academic offerings of a university, and its very high prestige has made it the queen of the social sciences. One reflection of its standing in academic circles has been the creation of special degrees, the Bachelor of Economics or the Bachelor of Commerce, which are now among the most popular choices at the Universities of Sydney and Melbourne, the largest universities in Australia. The emphasis given in Australia to the study of economics mirrors the country's very vital concern with questions of external trade, wage levels, industrial and agricultural development, population capacity, and full employment. These topics frequently command the nation's headlines, are the subject of political debate, and are directly the concern of the Commonwealth government and its employees.

The extent to which degrees in economics have been sought by officers of the Service is illustrated in the nature of the degrees obtained by holders of "free places." Out of the 147 degrees completed by 1952, 82 were in economics or commerce; and of the 48 diploma courses completed, 33 were for the diploma of commerce. Only 13 arts degrees were included (and some of these probably with majors in economics or other "practical" subjects).[34] The degrees sought by veterans under the Reconstruction Training Program have shown a similar pattern toward economics or other job-related subjects.[35]

Although the university recruitment scheme begun in 1934 was open to all graduates, and in fact initially attracted a majority of arts degrees (the scheme was halted after 1941), it is significant that by 1952 these early recruits were concentrated more in External Affairs than in any other department. This department is the only one in the Service in which a nonspecialized degree is explicitly valued. Moreover, the second largest group, with law degrees, was to be found in the Attorney-General's Department. Finally some of the arts graduates subsequent to their recruitment went on to attend a university on a part-time basis in order to earn more specialized degrees.

The evidence would seem to suggest the strong bias in the Service in favor of the officer who can demonstrate the immediate practical value of his

[34] The other degrees were science (24), engineering (8), and law (20). See Public Service Board, *Twenty-Eighth Report* (1952), p. 14.
[35] See Public Service Board, *Twenty-Fifth Report* (1949), p. 22.

education and training. It has been observed that historically the prestige of university attendance was never transplanted to Australia, and that the traditional emphasis of higher education has been upon professional training. Moreover, "Anyone who criticizes the Australian public service for not modelling its recruitment policy on the British should remember that no section of Australian commerce or industry accepted the Northcote-Trevelyan assumptions about the Arts graduate."[36] When the Commonwealth Service introduced the graduate scheme in the thirties, it was definitely charting new ground.

Reflecting and reinforcing the Australian bias toward the expert is the Public Service machinery itself. The whole system of personnel administration is heavily weighted to give preference to the officer who can demonstrate competence for a particular job. The classification system atomizes each position and stresses the particular competence required to perform a specific set of duties; and the promotion formula, with its emphasis upon "special qualification and aptitude," together with the appeals arrangement, gives a decided advantage to the officer who can demonstrate that his training and background suit him for the particular vacancy in question. For many years the accounting certificate constituted the most valuable qualification—there were at least sixty accounting certificates represented among the senior officers considered in this study who were appointed

[36] J.B.D. Miller, *Australian Government and Politics: An Introductory Survey* (London, 1954), p. 151.

between 1939 and 1952. This has now been supplemented by an appropriate university degree, a diploma in commerce or public administration, or by other concrete symbols of proficiency (e.g., aviation experience in the Civil Aviation Department, military rank or training in the defense departments, etc.). The system tends to perpetuate itself, one expert looking favorably upon an officer with similar training and quick to defend the interests of his profession. As one British observer has pointed out, it may not be long before the higher ranks of the Service will be open only to those with a degree or other formal qualifications—a situation which contrasts with the British Administrative Class, which is filled in part by promotion from below of officers without formal or academic training.[37]

An Assessment of Graduate Recruitment. The insertion of Section 36A in the Public Service Act in 1933 was the result of a compromise between the pressures from the university associations and the Public Service staff associations, the Board itself taking a somewhat equivocal position. The amendment was agreed to by the Board on an experimental basis and, it would seem, largely in consequence of

[37] C. J. Hayes, *Report on the Public Service Commissions of British Commonwealth Countries* (London, 1955), p. 6. For a strong attack against the weight given to symbols of proficiency, especially "pass" (below honor standard) degrees, and a discussion of other aspects of recruitment and promotion policies, see S. Encel, "Recruitment of University Graduates to the Commonwealth Public Service," *Public Administration*, Dec., 1953, pp. 222-231; and "The Commonwealth Public Service and Outside Recruitment," *Public Administration*, March, 1955, pp. 28-43.

the serious damage done to the Service by the recruitment policies of the twenties. According to the
Board, the object of the scheme was to "assist in
building up a reserve for filling the higher departmental positions, without interfering with the advancement of officers within the Service who may
demonstrate their fitness to undertake the higher
responsibilities of office."[38] The passage of the
amendment was accompanied by loud cries of protest
from the Clerical Association, an employee organization whose thinking has hardly kept pace with the
times and which therefore frequently displays evidence of having a vested interest in mediocrity. By
stressing the dangers of an "elite class" or privileged
few, and interpreting the Australian aphorism "fair
go" for all as "equal go" for all, this organization
and the segment of Public Service and political opinion which it represents appear to have been to a large
extent responsible for the inability of the Commonwealth Service to go beyond the experimental
provisions of the 1933 legislation. That the experiment was destined for only moderate success is
suggested by the very few suitable applications received prior to the war, and perhaps also by the
number of subsequent resignations.[39] It was probably
too much to hope that a system which made no
distinction for special ability could successfully accommodate the university graduate. As one critic
observed, "promotion under this scheme depends

[38] Public Service Board, *Sixth Report* (1929), p. 21.
[39] By 1952 nearly one-fourth of the seventy-four recruits appointed between 1934 and 1941 had resigned from the Service.

upon the performance of routine work," and "a university graduate can file correspondence and stamp cards no better than a boy of 16."[40]

Initially, what made Section 36A a *valuable* recruitment authorization was that its introduction happened to coincide with the creation of a diplomatic staff for which a good university degree was appropriate. More recently, however (the scheme commenced again in 1948), the section has been used to a large extent to bring into the Service the recruit whose university training qualifies him for one of the many rather specialized functions now performed in the Service. Graduates in economics, psychology, sociology, library science, as well as the graduates in the more technical faculties, can now find positions in the Service requiring their training. In effect, then, Section 36A together with the free place scheme and the cadet program has tended to become a supplement to the lateral recruitment provisions for the recruitment of the specialist into the Service, and its success in providing a "leaven of highly educated recruits" to assume "higher departmental positions" will probably depend upon the ability of the graduate to make use of his special competence to work his way up the hierarchy to positions which are primarily administrative or advisory. In some departments this pattern of advancement will likely prevail. In others, however, especially those having relatively few positions requiring university training and placing major emphasis on general administration (e.g., the Post

[40] Parker, p. 270.

Office, Customs and Excise, Territories, Social Services, and Interior), the graduate still has difficulty in making his way. He is resented by his colleagues and sometimes actually discriminated against because of his educational background. For these reasons some departments are generally wary of submitting requests to the Board for "36A" recruits.

Finally, Section 36A has been made into a *workable* recruitment authorization mainly in consequence of the ability of the Board, now alive to the vital functions which graduate recruitment can and must perform, to minimize the effects of the restrictive clauses. The intended quantitative restriction has been nullified through the appointment of veteran graduates under the veteran preference regulation, as well as by the peculiar phraseology of the 10 per cent clause itself.[41] And while graduates must still commence duty in a base-grade position, promotion to a position appropriate to his training is usually rapid; and sometimes the graduate—especially the ones who have been carefully selected by a department through its university contacts—begins immediately in an "acting" capacity in a higher office.

There are, in summary, at least three functions which graduate recruitment has fulfilled: the recruitment of diplomatic officers, the recruitment of specialists, and the provision of a corps of officers who, in some departments at least, may be expected to assume the higher positions. However, as a result of the evolution of the educational system the most

[41] See above p. 43.

important function of graduate recruitment in the future—one closely related to the others—will be to fulfil, at least in part, the role heretofore performed by the transfer and Leaving examinations. Whether the rather fortuitous solutions which thus far have minimized the restrictive legal provisions will permanently allow Section 36A to perform all these functions, and perform them well, remains uncertain. The problems of competing with industry and commerce, which now have also begun graduate recruitment, and of attracting the proper proportion of honors graduates still have to be faced.

CONCLUSION

Australia has unquestionably taken great strides in recent years towards the objective of a strong and efficient Public Service. Not only has it been able to fill its ranks with some of Australia's best talent, but in other ways has set for itself high goals. Progress has been made in spite of serious problems, some of which are similar to those facing public services throughout the world, others of which have resulted from past mistakes or from conditions peculiar to Australia.

In many ways the questions and problems facing Australia are similar to those which confront the United States in its consideration of a "senior civil service," recommended by the Second Hoover Commission in 1955. Both the Australian and United States Services are based on a similar classification concept, give wide scope to the specialist, and are founded on a strong and valuable egalitarian tradition. In both countries the question is how to adjust these practices and traditions with the needs of higher management and administration, and to make the adjustment amid strong pressures from employee organizations, departments, and other interested groups.

What distinguishes Australia from the United States, and from the United Kingdom as well, has been its failure to examine periodically its Public Service through a royal commission or other means. There would be dangers in such a course, since a serious investigation would probably entail disputes over federal-state relations, the role of government in the economy, and other contentious questions. Nevertheless, the long-range value might well outweigh any temporary discomfort. The growth of the Commonwealth Service has now leveled off, the functions of administration have been stabilized, and, most important, the public servant continues to play an extremely vital role in the life of the community. It is to an examination of this role that attention will now be focused.[42]

[42] On April 10, 1957, a Government announcement in the House of Representatives, while directed in part against those groups in Australia which have been calling for the appointment of a Hoover-type commission to investigate the Public Service, did affirm the value of inquiries into the Public Service machinery. Thus it was stated that the Government hoped to appoint a committee "to examine one most important section of Public Service machinery," the "recruitment standards and processes." It seems likely, therefore, that now, twenty-five years after the last major change in recruitment policy, new recruitment programs will be introduced.

5

The Role of the Higher Public Service

DETERMINING FACTORS

THE ROLE of the higher public servant in a parliamentary democracy is determined to a large extent by the degree of authority and control wielded by the legislative body, and by the ability of cabinet ministers to handle their portfolios with competence. In Australia several factors have combined to weaken control over administration either by ministers or by Parliament, and have consequently enhanced both the responsibility and the influence of the permanent official.

Ministers. One of the most important of these factors has been the frequent changes in portfolios, resulting both from the constitutional provision limiting the life of a Government to three years and from the general political instability which has characterized several ministries. The ministerial head has thus remained in charge of his department for relatively short periods of time, while the responsibility of the public servant has increased proportionately.

The extent to which the permanent official has been relied upon to provide administrative continuity is illustrated in Table VII.

TABLE VII
NUMBER OF MINISTERS OF STATE AND PERMANENT HEADS, 1901-1952*

DEPARTMENTS	MINISTERS	CHANGES IN PORTFOLIOS†	PERMANENT HEADS
Attorney-General's........	14	18	3
Defence.................	28	30	5
External Affairs, Home and Territories, Home Affairs, Interior...............	29	32	7
Home Affairs, Works and Railways..............	21	22	4
Postmaster-General's......	29	29	6
Treasury................	19	26	7
Trade and Customs.......	30	34	9
Prime Minister's..........	12	13	6
Health.................	17	20	3
Markets and Migration, Commerce, etc.........	12	12	5
External Affairs...........	11	11	4
Civil Aviation............	7	6	3
Social Services...........	6	5	1
Air....................	7	6	2
Army...................	6	5	1
Navy...................	8	7	2
Labour and National Service	7	8	3
Works..................	5	4	1
Immigration.............	2	1	1
Territories..............	5	4	2

*Certain wartime departments have been excluded, as well as certain departments created in the postwar period. Sources: Commonwealth of Australia, *Official Year Book*, No. 18 (1925), pp. 82-83; *ibid.*, No. 38 (1951), pp. 74-89; and *ibid.*, No. 39 (1953), pp. 79-88.
†Since the first appointment.

Another important factor has been the location of the federal capital. Most ministers whose departments have their central offices located in Canberra are rarely in close contact with any but the most senior officer, i.e., the permanent head, and spend little time actually working in their departments. For this the great distance which separates Canberra from local constituencies is partly responsible. Yet even when visiting Canberra during parliamentary sessions, most ministers have elected to place their offices in Parliament House, rather than in the departmental building—a practice which facilitates close contacts among ministers, but which also isolates the official from the center of political direction.

One observer has discussed the responsibility of the Commonwealth permanent heads by contrasting them with their counterparts in the states:

Generally speaking, Commonwealth ministers take a less active part in the actual administration of their departments than do ministers of State governments; and Commonwealth permanent heads are accustomed to carrying a heavier burden of responsibility, even for policy, than the corresponding State officials. At the same time, the doctrine of ministerial responsibility has been most sedulously cultivated in Commonwealth circles; and, before the war, rather less co-ordination was imposed on individual ministers and their departments by the Prime Minister than was customary in most State governments. The position of permanent head of a Commonwealth department is accordingly one of great power, and the personnel of the higher grades of the civil service is a most important factor in the life of the Australian nation.[1]

Coupled with short tenure and their isolation from administration, ministers are selected for quali-

[1] E. Ronald Walker, *The Australian Economy in War and Reconstruction* (New York, 1947), p. 109.

ties of which administrative competence is not always the most important. H. E. Dale, writing of the higher civil servants in Great Britain, notes that at Westminster competition for cabinet rank is so keen that M.P.'s of proved ability are usually selected.[2] In Australia, by way of contrast, when a Labour Government is in office, the composition of the ministry is determined by a vote of the parliamentary caucus;[3] and while the leader of a Liberal-Country Coalition is not hampered by the formal institution of a caucus, his choice of ministers is strictly limited by the nature of the agreement reached between the two parties.

Furthermore, until the enactment of the 1948 Representation Act the field of selection for cabinet responsibility was limited by the restricted size of Parliament—seventy-four members in the House and thirty-six in the Senate. It was noted by one critic that as the number of portfolios increased without corresponding increases in the size of Parliament, a portion of the ministry tended to be weak. "Under such circumstances," he observed, "the Prime Minister has to leave the 'tail' in the care of its Departmental officers or himself undertake the essential stimulation and energising."[4]

Another factor which has tended to lower the standard of ministerial ability has been the hesitancy

[2] H. E. Dale, *The Higher Civil Service of Great Britain* (London, 1941), p. 112.

[3] The Prime Minister himself, however, distributes the portfolios.

[4] L. F. Crisp, *The Parliamentary Government of the Commonwealth of Australia* (New Haven, 1949), p. 203.

of successive Governments to adopt the practice of appointing parliamentary undersecretaries and thus prepare junior party members for future cabinet responsibility. Although the experiment has been tried on occasion, the practice has not become an accepted one. Militating against the use of undersecretaries is the constitutional provision that no one, unless he be a minister of state, can hold an office of profit under the Crown and remain a member of Parliament.[5] The failure of Parliament to constitute a system of standing committees on which members might become competent in certain fields of administration has also made it inevitable that the minister enters his office with little knowledge of matters of his department. In summary:

. . . the Australian cabinet minister, even now, is primarily a loyal party worker and only rarely a man of brilliant performance in scholarship, business, the professions and other non-political occupations. He is a skilled politician and wields power in his party; he will probably make a good showing in parliament, whose ways he knows from long experience; but it is only rarely that he is a man of sufficient personal distinction to impose himself upon his permanent advisers and make himself master of his Department. Usually he is only too glad of the weight of expert knowledge behind him.[6]

The nearness of this "expert knowledge" in moments of policy decision and parliamentary debate supports this observation. In 1939 when the Cabinet

[5] Section 44 (iv).
[6] J. B. D. Miller, *Australian Government and Politics: An Introductory Survey* (London, 1954), p. 147.

met in Hobart, some sixty ministers and officials are reported to have traveled to the meeting;[7] and it is only very recently that the large number of public servants who formerly attended the meetings of cabinet committees have been excluded. Yet officials still remain close to the minister in Parliament, and the minister places heavy reliance on the valuable notes and whispered comments which flow from his official aides.

Parliament. Without minimizing the role which the public official plays in the functioning of modern parliamentary government, it remains true that Parliament can still retain a significant control over administration and the bureaucracy. "The responsibility of ministers to Parliament means that every decision, even if it is taken far down in the official hierarchy, may be criticised by Parliament. . . . Ministers must not make mistakes; therefore civil servants must not make mistakes."[8]

In Australia Parliament has appeared reluctant to exercise the means of control which are open to it. Partly responsible has been the relative infrequency of parliamentary sessions and the consequent limitations upon the members' opportunity to question and criticize. For the period 1937-1947, half of which was under Liberal-Country Governments and half

[7] Crisp, p. 214.

[8] W. Ivor Jennings, *The British Constitution* (Cambridge, 1941), pp. 133-134. For a viewpoint which minimizes parliamentary influence see Ramsay Muir, *How Britain Is Governed* (New York, 1930), chap. ii.

under Labour Governments, the number of sittings of the House of Representatives was as follows:[9]

In 1937 the House sat on 35 days spread over 11 weeks
In 1938 the House sat on 66 days spread over 22 weeks
In 1939 the House sat on 51 days spread over 15 weeks
In 1940 the House sat on 43 days spread over 15 weeks
In 1941 the House sat on 50 days spread over 20 weeks
In 1942 the House sat on 45 days spread over 17 weeks
In 1943 the House sat on 48 days spread over 16 weeks
In 1944 the House sat on 57 days spread over 17 weeks
In 1945 the House sat on 90 days spread over 26 weeks
In 1946 the House sat on 65 days spread over 19 weeks
In 1947 the House sat on 65 days spread over 26 weeks

Nor has Parliament when in session made effective use of the possible instruments at its disposal to control administration. It has failed to organize a system of standing committees to inquire into legislative problems or administrative practices, and from 1932 to 1953 it suspended the operation of the one important committee which had been formed, the Joint Committee of Public Accounts. Royal commissions, too, are infrequent, as the example of the Public Service itself fully illustrates. Perhaps most surprising of all, only two regular departments (Social Services and the Post Office) are required to submit annual reports of their operations.[10] Thus

[9] This table was presented by F. A. Bland, "The Working of Parliamentary Government in Australia," *Parliamentary Affairs*, Winter, 1950, p. 78. Figures for more recent periods come close to the prewar pattern.

[10] The Repatriation Department and the Taxation Branch of the Treasury, both administered by specially appointed commissioners, also submit annual reports. Also some departments

the occasions when the senior official is called upon to render account to Parliament are few. Furthermore, although Parliament has made extensive use of the device of delegated legislation, it has not attempted to exercise effective scrutiny over the promulgation of administrative regulations.

Under the able chairmanship of Professor F. A. Bland, who for many years held the chair of Public Administration at Sydney University, the Parliamentary Joint Committee of Public Accounts has, since 1953, helped to restore to some extent Parliament's rightful interest in expenditure and administration. Already his committee has shed light on many important administrative problems, and for the first time in their careers many senior officials are being asked to justify, explain, and interpret activities of their departments.

Federalism. Another factor which may be mentioned as having fixed the role of the senior official is Australian federalism. Commonwealth-state relationships, on both the political and administrative levels, are, by their nature, complicated, and the joint policy-making and administrative machinery which has been developed has thrust upon the Commonwealth official tasks which might normally have been reserved for the politician. In the field of financial relationships, in particular, the "technical" matters referred to public servants have tended to disguise

---

are required to report annually on the administration of certain acts, e.g., the Attorney-General's Department on the Bankruptcy Act.

the inability of political leaders to agree among themselves. It has been noted that "conferences of experts are coming to be an accessory feature of Premiers' Conferences themselves; the Premiers decide a principle, set their experts to fight out details, and then adopt the result."[11]

Recent trends. Recent developments which have affected the role of the public official have already been suggested. Expressed in quantitative terms, his increased responsibility is reflected in the percentage of the national income spent by the Government he serves. In 1938-1939 this amounted to 8.3 per cent; in 1954-1955, 15.1 per cent. Including the annual grants to the states, the percentages were 10.3 and 20.1, respectively.[12] Of greater significance is the type of function to which the higher public servant now devotes his energies. The complexity of modern government has thrown into new relief the responsibility which must, of necessity, be borne by the permanent official, and by stressing the primacy of policy over *ad hoc* administrative decisions has given new urgency to his role in planning, advising, and coordinating.[13] The higher public servant has also tended to become an integral part of the government machinery rather than an employee of a single depart-

[11] Geoffrey Sawer, *Australian Government Today* (4th ed., Melbourne, 1954), p. 10.

[12] Figures taken from Commonwealth Parliament, *National Income and Expenditure, 1954-55* (1955).

[13] A valuable account of some of these complexities as seen by a permanent secretary is J. G. Crawford, "The Role of the Permanent Head," *Public Administration*, Sept., 1954, pp. 153-165.

ment. The number of overseas conferences he must attend, together with the boards, commissions, and interdepartmental and Commonwealth-state committees on which he must serve, has meant that many senior officers have become roving delegates, rather than stationary administrators.[14]

AUSTRALIAN ATTITUDE TOWARD THE ROLE OF THE PUBLIC SERVANT

In contrast to the United Kingdom, Australia lacks a strong tradition which stresses the valuable and honorable role of the public official in the determination of matters of government policy. Public opinion generally has been loath to affirm that the official can do more than respond obediently to the directives issued by the political representatives of the electorate. Thus when Prime Minister Lyons first suggested that a senior public servant be admitted to cabinet meetings to act as secretary, the proposal was regarded as "something like a constitutional revolution."[15] More recently this attitude has been expressed in the numerous attacks upon the new Commonwealth "bureaucracy," as illustrated by the comments by two Australian economists on the "Bureaucratic Revolution":

The professional Public Servant has gradually assumed economic and political power, power over private enterprise and power over even the unions. He has

[14] The practice of appointing Treasury representatives to various statutory bodies is critically examined in Joint Committee of Public Accounts, *Twenty-First Report* (1955), para. 141-150.

[15] Crisp, p. 214.

taken over the control of the running of the country because of the increasing complexity of the job and because of the decreasing ability of the ordinary politician to cope with it. . . . A few years ago a new Federal Government called for a plan to restore free enterprise, abolish controls, and cut down the cost of Government. This was completely opposed to the very spirit of the Revolution. No help came from the Public Service planners and the Government had to struggle on as best it could with very little alteration to the previous system of a tightly controlled economy.[16]

Reinforcing this basic hostility is the peculiar nature of the federal capital. It is isolated from the main concourse of events, and its populace is composed mostly of public servants and their families. It is largely an artificial community. The public servant in Canberra, therefore, is in danger of losing touch with the community he is intended to serve; he is insulated from the criticism, warnings, and feelings of the individuals and groups which would be found in one of the larger urban areas.

Whatever the explanation, attacks on the "bureaucracy" are frequent, and the Public Service Board has felt obliged to defend the role of the senior official. In its 1952 report the Board explained:

It would be idle to deny the important place which senior officials hold in advising Ministers and Governments on the formation of policy. This does not affect

[16] Colin Clark and W. H. Herbert, quoted from a paper read before the 1953 Winter School of the Australian Institute of Political Science. The paper was reported in part in the *Sydney Morning Herald*, July 19, 1953, p. 5.

the fact that responsibility for policy rests with the Government and not with the official. This position has never been in doubt but it has tended to become confused in certain public criticisms in recent times.[17]

PUBLIC SERVICE NEUTRALITY

Ministerial-Official Relationship. Once it is conceded that the public servant, because of his intimate acquaintance with the problems of his department, is expected to cultivate ideas and opinions of his own— that he is, in other words, to be more than "a movable piece of office furniture"[18]—then there arises the question of establishing a corps of senior officers which can command the respect of any Government or minister who may be returned to office. Since the war two dramatic episodes concerning the Department of External Affairs illustrate the fact that the responsibility for maintaining a sound ministerial-official relationship rests both with the minister and with the public official himself.

While Dr. H. V. Evatt was Minister for External Affairs, several officers of his department, on both the junior and senior level, either resigned from the Service or sought transfer to another department.

[17] Public Service Board, *Twenty-Eighth Report* (1952), p. 6. It has been observed that both in office and in opposition non-Labour Governments "have in the world of commerce, finance and primary and secondary industry many sources of very important information and advice on which they can draw. . . ," and consequently are less ready than a Labour Government to rely upon official advice. See Canberra Research Group, "Commonwealth Policy Co-ordination," *Public Administration*, Dec., 1955, p. 200.

[18] A phrase used by Herman Finer, *The British Civil Service* (London, 1937), p. 187.

The reasons underlying the discontent were suggested by Mr. Paul Hasluck in a speech delivered shortly after his resignation in 1947 as Australian representative on the United Nations Security Council. Mr. Hasluck explained that, in his view, Dr. Evatt wished "to make the diplomatic staff and the staff of the Department of External Affairs his personal possession." In "his eagerness to advance Australia by his own dynamic impact on world affairs," Hasluck charged, "he is tending to bend to his own use and own purposes a service which itself has continuing responsibilities. . . ." Then in an illuminating passage Mr. Hasluck stated his conception of the proper role of the public servant:

By reason of his continuity in office, his expertness, and his opportunities for gathering information and studying it—an opportunity which no Minister has—the higher officer of the Public Service may be able to make a valuable contribution in the early and formative stages of policy-making. The late John Curtin, with whom I once talked on this subject, shared such views and I know placed a considerable value on the information and advice that a public servant in my own department and in other departments could give faithfully to Minister after Minister, informing them impartially, showing them what they had overlooked, and presenting arguments against as well as for a proposition right up to the point at which the Minister was ready to take the decision for which he alone could accept responsibility in Parliament. Once the decision is made the Service is bound to carry out the policy, but up to that point it has the full right and duty to give without reserve and without faltering whatever it has learnt from experience or study.

Finally, Mr. Hasluck concluded that "if any attempt is made to exercise close control over a department in such a way as to make a department the acquiescent echo of a Minister's will, then the Service is being debased."[19]

Two years after the resignation of Mr. Hasluck, the External Affairs Department was again the scene of an episode which centered on the relationship between minister and senior official. This time, however, the controversial action was that of the public servant, and the issue that of his right to stand for parliamentary election.

Until 1945 a public servant was restrained by provisions of the Constitution and the Electoral Act from standing for parliamentary election. According to Section 44 of the Constitution, any person who "Holds any office of profit under the Crown . . . shall be incapable of being chosen or of sitting as a senator or a member of the House of Representatives"; and the Electoral Act required that any person nominated as a senator or member of the House must be qualified under the Constitution to be so elected. An officer could, of course, have resigned from the Service while seeking election and, if defeated, have applied for reappointment under Section 46 of the Public Service Act (appointment of retired

[19] *Sydney Morning Herald*, Sept. 10, 1947, p. 4; and *Parliamentary Debates*, Sept. 24, 1947, Vol. 193, pp. 178-179 (where Mr. Hasluck's speech was quoted at length by Mr. Menzies). Mr. Hasluck is now a Liberal party minister.

officers). In doing so, however, he would have surrendered all of his accumulated rights. It was to correct this disadvantage that the Labour party in 1945 sponsored an amendment to the Public Service Act which granted to every public servant the right to resign from the Service in order to seek parliamentary honors and, if defeated, to return to the Service with exactly the same status as he had prior to resignation.[20]

Perhaps encouraged by this liberalization of the Public Service Act, the permanent head of the Department of External Affairs, Dr. John Burton, early in 1949 offered himself as a candidate for nomination by the Labour party. One of the first graduates to be recruited to the Service in 1937, Burton had served as private secretary to the Minister for External Affairs, Dr. Evatt, and after a meteoric rise had been appointed Secretary of the External Affairs Department in 1947. He sought the Labour party nomination to contest the parliamentary seat for the Australian Capital Territory. Because this political contest was confined to the one party, and was not an open election, Burton was not compelled to resign from the Service. He remained in office, therefore, and when defeated for the nomination continued to serve as secretary of the department.

During the course of the supply debate a few months later, the Leader of the Opposition, Mr. Menzies, announced that if his party were returned

<hr>

[20] Commonwealth Public Service Act, Act No. 43, 1945.

to office he would not tolerate Dr. Burton as head of External Affairs:

Suppose that . . . I find myself Minister for External Affairs. I shall be met, on my first morning, by the permanent head of the Department of External Affairs who has pledged himself publicly to defeat me and who, but for the accident of his non-selection, would have been a candidate against a member of my party at the elections. . . . I could not have any confidence in the advice of a head of a department in those circumstances, and I would not tolerate him as a head of a department.[21]

Within seven months the Menzies Government was returned to power. Dr. Burton retained his position for six months, was then given a six-month leave of absence, and finally in early 1951 was appointed Australian High Commissioner to Ceylon. Although the Government never issued an official explanation for the appointment of the new secretary, there is no reason to doubt that the action was directly linked with Burton's previous political activities.[22]

The Problem of Neutrality. Even granted that the public official scrupulously abides by the conventions which govern political activity, the question

---

[21] *Parliamentary Debates*, June 8, 1949, Vol. 202, p. 670.

[22] Not long after his arrival in Colombo, Dr. Burton returned to Sydney and won the Labour party nomination for Lowe (a Sydney seat) for the double dissolution election in April, 1951. By this time he had submitted his resignation from the Service. Defeated in the election, Burton did not apply for reappointment to the Service.

Related to the question of neutrality is the problem of public servant participation in academic discussion. See L. C. Webb, "Academic Freedom and the Civil Services," *Public Administration*, March, 1954, pp. 57-61.

still remains as to whether a public servant can effectively administer the program of a Government whose policies conflict with his personal inclinations or philosophy. Is it essential, as it appears to be in Washington, that the political beliefs of the top official be in sympathy with those of his political chief?

This question has never been squarely faced in Australia.[23] The Commonwealth Service was founded upon the British tradition of permanent tenure, and until 1939 it functioned successfully in providing for the Government of the day a coterie of senior officials capable of administering the limited functions of the Commonwealth. Because of the nature of these functions, the personal beliefs of the officers were of little consequence and never became the subject of serious discussion. But under present-day conditions, when public servants are heavily involved in national planning and economic controls, the nature of the beliefs held by certain senior officials becomes more relevant, and the question arises as to the limits of neutrality which should be or can be expected.

It was probably not accidental that the Department of Post-war Reconstruction, established in 1942 as the first full-fledged planning department of the Service, was staffed by some well-known supporters of the Labour party and advocates of economic plan-

[23] In the United Kingdom the question has been discussed in connection with the social composition of the Administrative Class. See, for example, Harold J. Laski, *Parliamentary Government in England* (London, 1938), chap. vi; and J. Donald Kingsley, *Representative Bureaucracy* (Yellow Springs, Ohio, 1944).

ning. Although on the whole these officers abided by the tradition of public service neutrality, there was little question of the direction in which their sympathies lay. It might, of course, be argued that these appointments represented a return to patronage, yet neither the press nor the Opposition attempted to make this charge. Or it might be contended that the nature of the department demanded a type of public servant which could be obtained solely from the ranks of university graduates, which include a large number of Labour supporters. But what seems as likely an explanation is that the minister deliberately staffed the department with men who were in sympathy with its objectives and who therefore could tackle their assignments with zeal.

Though the Department of Post-war Reconstruction was formally abolished in 1950, its personnel still remain scattered throughout the ranks of the Service, many of them occupying highly responsible positions. Other senior officers, moreover, in such important departments as the Treasury, which experienced rapid growth and reorganization during the period 1941-1949, were appointed to their posts during Labour's reign in office. Since the coming to power of the Liberal-Country Government in 1949, therefore, the question has been raised by certain backbenchers and by the press as to whether a Liberal-Country program can be executed successfully by these officials who were left behind by the Labour Government. Typical of the doubts which have been expressed is that by one Liberal backbencher during the debate on the budget introduced by his party in 1951: "That it is a socialist Budget is inevitable. When the Labour Government was overthrown in 1949, it left behind in the top Public Service positions a large corps of advisers who had been selected for their socialist tendencies as well as their own qualifications."[24]

Regardless of the validity of these charges, what is of outstanding significance is the fact that the new Government has made no attempt to remove these officials or to flood the Service with officers of its own choosing. No doubt this is in part a reflection of the practical limits within which a new Government may alter the policies initiated by the old. Furthermore, it may be noted that while there have been few significant staff changes, the new Government has not been prevented from relying upon officials other than those who appear to have been the major architects of Labour policy. But the fact that the system of permanent tenure has withstood successfully the pressures which have arisen during the period of the welfare state has been an achievement of no mean significance and reflects the inherent strength in Australia of the British tradition of public service stability and neutrality.[25]

[24] *Parliamentary Debates*, Oct. 23, 1951, Vol. 214, p. 1006.
[25] The victory of Canada's Progressive Conservative party in June, 1957, will give this Commonwealth country an opportunity to test the strength of its tradition of tenure for senior civil servants. From 1935, and throughout the period in which momentous changes affected the role of government, the Liberal party had held office. Writing in 1955, J. E. Hodgetts posed the problem this way: "Skilled resources of the civil service

In summary, the senior official in Australia performs a function very similar to that entrusted to the Administrative Class in Great Britain. He is a permanent and integral part of the government machine who by virtue of his *expertise* and aloofness from political strife is able to provide successive Governments with information, advice, and the continual benefit of his experience. Australian opinion does not appear ready to accept the full implications of the valuable role which the public servant can, and does, perform; and the recent events in the Department of External Affairs suggest that the basic problems surrounding the relationships between the minister and the senior official may not yet be completely solved. Nevertheless, the basic similarity between British and Australian practice is apparent, and in both countries the permanent civil servant remains the core around which the workings of parliamentary democracy revolve.

---

will prevent those blunders which usually bring about the political downfall of a Government; meanwhile, the long tenure of permanent officials under an unchanging dominant party produces an identification of interest and outlook; finally, the solid corps of senior officials looks complacently into a common mirror and receives an acceptable answer to the collective question 'Who is now the fairest in the land?' " See "The Liberal and the Bureaucrat," *Queen's Quarterly*, Summer, 1955, pp. 182-183.

SELECT BIBLIOGRAPHY

I. OFFICIAL COMMONWEALTH PUBLICATIONS

The following is a select list of the most useful Commonwealth documents and serial publications relating to the Commonwealth Public Service:

(a) *Statutes, Regulations, Arbitration Reports*
Commonwealth Public Service Act 1902-1918
Commonwealth Public Service Act 1922-1954
Arbitration (Public Service) Act 1920-1952
Commonwealth Public Service Regulations:
  Regulations under the Public Service Act are published in the *Commonwealth of Australia Gazette*, the annual volumes of *Commonwealth Statutory Rules*, and in compilations published by the Public Service Board.
Commonwealth Public Service Determinations:
  The determinations, which rest on a legal basis slightly different from that of the regulations, relate to conditions of promotion and qualifications for particular positions. The determinations are published by the Board and consolidated at irregular intervals.

Commonwealth Public Service Arbitration Reports. Determinations made and interpretations given pursuant to the Arbitration (Public Service) Act. Published in annual volumes.

(b) *Reports of the Public Service Commissioner and Board*

Commonwealth Public Service Commissioner, *Reports*, 1-18 (1903-4—1921-22)

Commonwealth Public Service Board, *Reports*, 1-31 (1923-24—1954-55)

The annual *Reports* of the Board are issued as separate documents and also are included in the compiled volumes of *Parliamentary Papers*.

(c) *Reports of Special Commissions of Inquiry*

Report on the Business Management of the Post-master-General's Department (Anderson), 1915. *Parliamentary Papers*, Session 1914-15-16-17, Vol. IV, pp. 341-381.

Royal Commission on Economies, 1920-21. Various reports in *Parliamentary Papers*, Session 1920-21.

Report of Royal Commission on Public Service Administration (McLachlan), 1920. *Parliamentary Papers*, Session 1920-21, Vol. IV, pp. 1525-1620.

Report of Committee of Inquiry into Systems of Promotion and Temporary Transfers (Government Printer, Canberra, 1945). This report was not included in the *Parliamentary Papers*.

Committee of Review, "Civil Staffing of Wartime Activities" (J. T. Pinner, A. A. Fitzgerald, *et al.*), 1945, unpublished report.

(d) *Other Serials*

Commonwealth Parliament, Joint Committee of Public Accounts, *Reports*, 1-26 (1953-1956). The first report of the revived Committee was published in 1953; by the end of 1956 a total of twenty-eight reports had been published. The reports are included in the *Parliamentary Papers*.

The Federal Guide, a handbook on the organization and functions of the Commonwealth government departments. Issued irregularly by the Prime Minister's Department.

II. BOOKS

The most complete treatments of the prewar public services in Australia, at both the Commonwealth and state level, are to be found in F. A. Bland, *Government in Australia* (2nd ed., Sydney, 1944), and Robert S. Parker, *Public Service Recruitment in Australia* (Melbourne, 1942). Bland's volume is a collection of public documents which relate to public administration, with special emphasis upon the public services. An introductory essay by the author sets the material in perspective. Since many of the documents included in the collection are difficult to obtain, the volume serves as a useful reference source. The study by Parker is a critical analysis of public service administration, with special attention being given to recruitment policy. The volume remains the most complete survey of the development of the Australian public services up to World War II.

Three books on Australian government contain good descriptions and appraisals of the Commonwealth Public Service. These are L. F. Crisp, *The Parliamentary Government of the Commonwealth of Australia* (New Haven, 1949), Chapter IX; J. B. D. Miller, *Australian Government and Politics: An Introductory Survey* (London, 1954), Chapter VII; and Paul Hasluck, *The Government and the People, 1939-1941* (Canberra, 1952), Chapter XI. The chapter by Hasluck, an official war historian, is particularly useful for its informative discussion of all phases of administration during World War II.

C. J. Hayes, *Report on the Public Service Commissions of the British Commonwealth* (London, 1955) is a useful handbook which outlines the public services of the Dominions. The author is an officer of the British Civil Service Commission. Chapter I is devoted to the Commonwealth and states of Australia.

III. JOURNAL ARTICLES

Most of the writing on the Commonwealth Public Service, and the state public services as well, has been done by public servants or former public servants. The writings are generally contained in *Public Administration,* the journal of the Australian Regional Groups of the Royal Institute of Public Administration, published in Sydney; occasional articles may also be found in *Public Administration,* the journal of the Royal Institute of Public Administration, published in London. Many of the articles published in the Australian journal are speeches or papers which have been presented to one of the state regional groups. With the establishment of the Canberra Regional Group in 1953, *Public Administration* (Sydney) may be expected to devote somewhat greater attention than in the past to matters relating to Commonwealth administration.

The following is a select list of the articles relating to the Commonwealth Public Service which have appeared since 1945. Except where noted, reference to *Public Administration* denotes the Australian journal.

J. J. Betts, "The Training of Commonwealth Public Servants," *Public Administration*, VIII (June-September, 1949), 70-79.

Leo Blair, "Arbitration in the Federal Public Service of Australia," *Public Administration* (London), XXXIV (Spring, 1956), 61-73.

———, "Employer-Employee Relationships in the Federal Public Service of Australia," *Public Administration* (London), XXXV (Spring, 1957), 53-63.

F. A. Bland, "Government Finance and the People: Control of Government Expenditure," *Public Administration*, XIV (June, 1955), 107-112.

Canberra Research Group, "Commonwealth Policy Co-ordination," *Public Administration*, XIV (December, 1955), 193-213.

J. G. Crawford, "The Role of the Permanent Head," *Public Administration*, XIII (September, 1954), 153-165.

E. E. Crichton, "The Development of Public Service Arbitration," *Public Administration*, XV (June, 1956), 150-166; (September, 1956), 214-231; (December, 1956), 319-333.

P. W. E. Curtin, "Commonwealth-State Relations: Administration," *Public Administration*, XII (June, 1953), 86-91.

S. R. Davis, "The Problem of Overlapping and Duplication between Commonwealth and State Public Services in Australia," *Public Administration*, X (September-December, 1951), 497-515.

S. Encel, "Recruitment of University Graduates to the Commonwealth Public Service," *Public Administration*, XII (December, 1953), 222-231.

————, "The Commonwealth Public Service and Outside Recruitment," *Public Administration*, XIV (March, 1955), 28-43.

A. A. Fitzgerald, "Public Administration and Democracy: Limits of Administrative Efficiency in a Democracy," *Public Administration*, XIII (March, 1954), 7-12.

K. E. Grainger, "O & M in the Commonwealth Public Service," *Public Administration*, XII (June, 1953), 65-84.

F. C. Green, "Changing Relations between Parliament and the Executive," *Public Administration*, XIII (June, 1954), 65-75.

Richard Griffiths, "The Role of the British Civil Servant in Policy Formation," *Public Administration*, XIV (September, 1955), 129-145.

B. W. Hartnell, "Current Problems in Commonwealth Administration," *Public Administration*, XII (December, 1953), 201-207.

————, "Power and Responsibility in the Commonwealth Public Service," *Public Administration*, XIV (September, 1955), 129-145.

T. H. Kewley, "Recent Developments in the Work of the Australian Commonwealth Public Service Board,"

Public Administration (London), XXVII (Winter, 1949), 269-277.

S. M. McKeon, "Public Administration and Democracy: Parliamentary Control of Departments," *Public Administration*, XIII (March, 1954), 13-18.

R. S. Parker, "Executive Development in the Commonwealth Public Service," *Public Administration*, XV (September, 1956), 177-198.

Howard A. Scarrow, "Further Comments upon the Recruitment of University Graduates to the Commonwealth Public Service," *Public Administration*, XIII (September, 1954), 166-175.

L. C. Webb, "Academic Freedom and the Civil Service," *Public Administration*, XIII (March, 1954), 57-61.

H. J. Wright, "Recent Developments in Administrative Training in the Commonwealth Public Service," *Public Administration*, XIII (September, 1954), 176-191.

INDEX